THE GOLEM'S MIGHTY SWING

BY JAMES STURM

DRAWN & QUARTERLY

The Golem's Mighty Swing was originally published in 2001, and collected in *James Sturm's America* in 2007.

drawnandquarterly.com

First edition: May 2017
Printed in China
10 9 8 7 6 5 4 3 2 1

Library and Archives Canada Cataloguing in Publication
Sturm, James, 1965–, author, illustrator
The Golem's Mighty Swing/James Sturm.
ISBN 978-1-77046-283-0 (paperback)
1. Graphic novels. I. Title.
PN6727.S78G65 2017 741.5'973 C2016-906238-4

Published in the USA by Drawn & Quarterly, a client publisher of Farrar, Straus and Giroux. Orders: 888.330.8477

Published in Canada by Drawn & Quarterly, a client publisher of Raincoast Books. Orders: 800.663.5714

Published in the United Kingdom by Drawn & Quarterly, a client publisher of Publishers Group UK. Orders: info@pguk.co.uk

ACKNOWLEDGMENTS

The work of baseball historian Donald Honig, cartoonist Ray Gotto,
and the Shonen Champion manga were valuable reference
in the production of *The Golem's Mighty Swing*.

Thank you Rachel, for everything.

In loving memory of Judith Dane.

THE GOLEM'S MIGHTY SWING: AN INTRODUCTION

by **Gene Luen Yang**

I bought a copy of James Sturm's *The Golem's Mighty Swing* in 2001, right when it was first published. I found it at an alternative comics convention. Back then, any comic book that didn't have capes or tights was automatically labeled alternative. A graphic novel about a Jewish baseball team in the 1920s? That was about as alternative as alternative got.

I finished *The Golem's Mighty Swing* in one sitting. Then I read it again. And again.

In a lecture that he gave a few years later, James described the comics medium as the intersection of poetry and graphic design. That's exactly what I encountered on those pages—a master poet and a master graphic designer melded into one cartoonist.

Sixteen years have passed, and the American comic book industry couldn't

be more different. The *New York Times*'s graphic books bestseller list, which didn't even exist in 2001, is dominated by stories about pretty much everything but capes and tights. A graphic novel about a Jewish baseball team in the 1920s no longer seems as alternative as it once did.

James Sturm played a huge role in these developments, not only as a cartoonist but also as a teacher. In addition to *The Golem's Mighty Swing*, he's written and drawn a number of beautifully-crafted graphic novels, including *Satchel Paige: Striking Out Jim Crow* and *Market Day*. He also founded The Center for Cartoon Studies, the nation's premiere comics-centric college.

The American comic book industry is very different. America is very different, too.

Today, America is in the throes of an identity crisis. Many Americans (as well as those who share the planet with Americans) are questioning the very soul of our country. Who are we, exactly? What do we stand for? And where are we going?

In times like this, it is helpful to be reminded of who we used to be, what we once stood for, and where we've been. And that is why *The Golem's Mighty Swing* is more timely now than when it was first released.

James shows us what America wishes it had been, and what America actually was. By rubbing the rose tint from our memories, he uncovers our nation's truest self.

We might want American history—and especially American sports history—to be a tidy collection of fables with easy-to-grasp morals. What we actually find is grittier and muddier, but perhaps still hopeful.

The America James reveals is the huckster who buys your culture from you, polishes off the rough spots, and sells it for a profit. America is the town loon who staggers through the streets warning of the doom that the strangers will bring.

But America is also the outsider who stands at the entrance of a cage, dressed in a ludicrous costume, ready to defend to the death a group of teammates who don't look anything like him.

America is a destroyer. But America is also our companion and our protector.

America is the golem.

—GENE LUEN YANG
Author of *American Born Chinese* and *The Shadow Hero*

BASEBALL

World's Champion Traveling Baseball Team!

STARS OF DAVID

THE BEARDED WANDERING WONDERS

VS

FOREST GROVE SPARTANS

FRIDAY, AUGUST 16

ADMISSION 50¢ 3:00 P.M.

THREE YEAR RECORD
1919 Won 110, Tied 3 of 162 Games
1920 Won 92, Tied 4 of 143 Games
1921 Won 136, Tied 1 of 160 Games
Average 20,000 Miles by Autobus Each Year

A REAL PARK PACKING ATTRACTION

RESERVED SEATING FOR WHITES

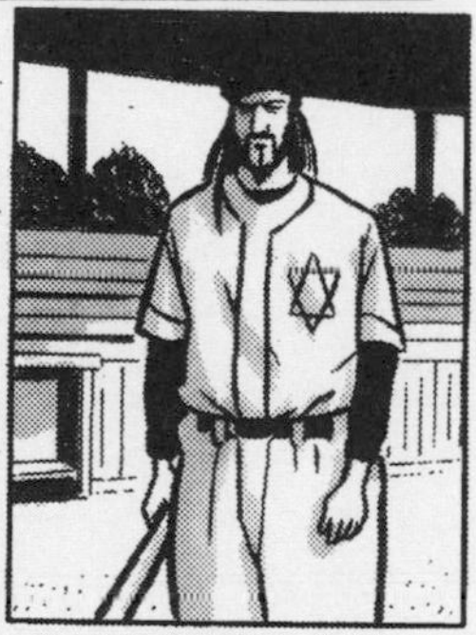

Formerly of the Boston Red Sox
Noah Strauss "The Zion Lion"

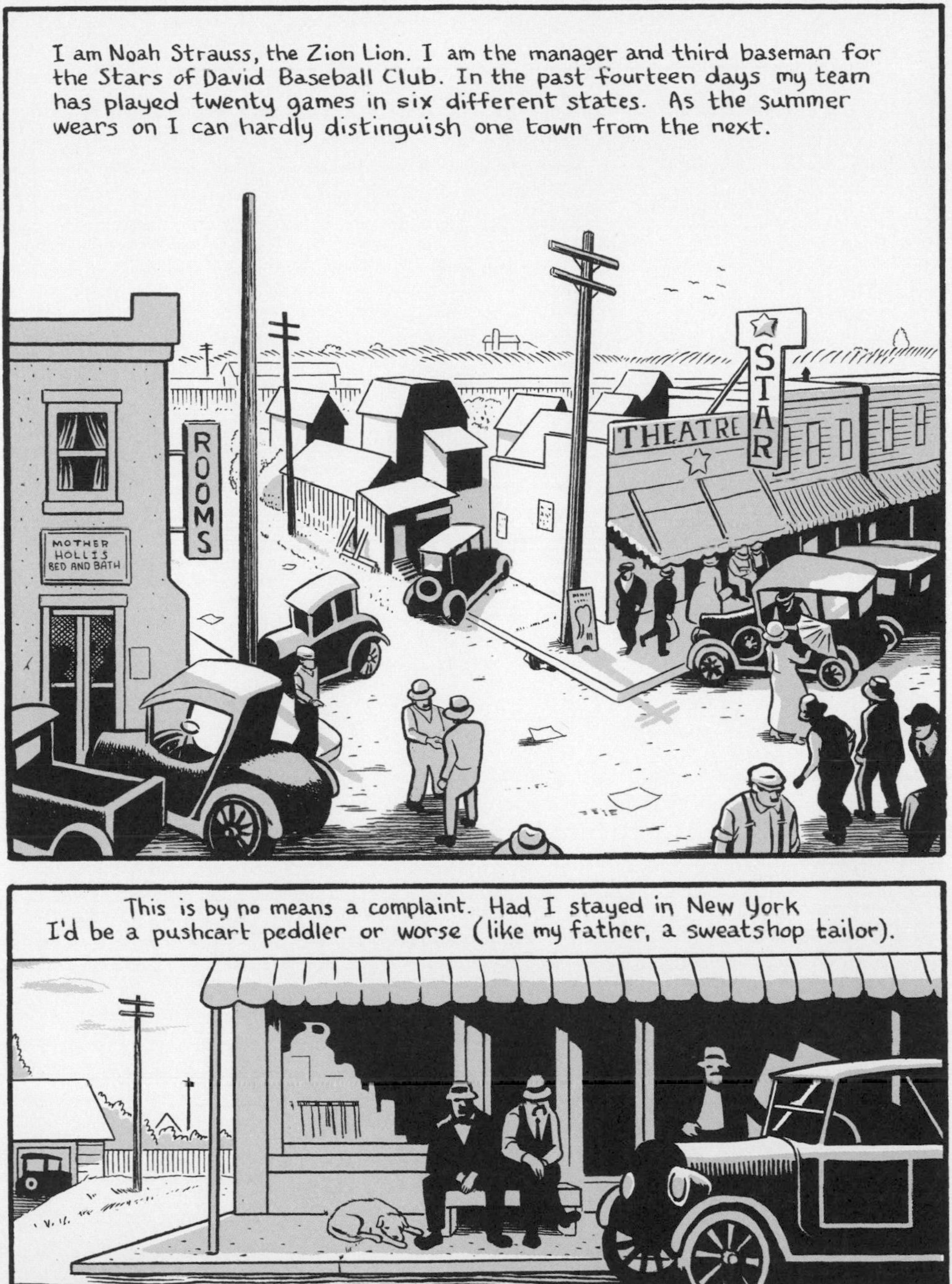
I am Noah Strauss, the Zion Lion. I am the manager and third baseman for the Stars of David Baseball Club. In the past fourteen days my team has played twenty games in six different states. As the summer wears on I can hardly distinguish one town from the next.
ROOMS
MOTHER HOLLIS BED AND BATH
THEATRE
STAR
This is by no means a complaint. Had I stayed in New York I'd be a pushcart peddler or worse (like my father, a sweatshop tailor).

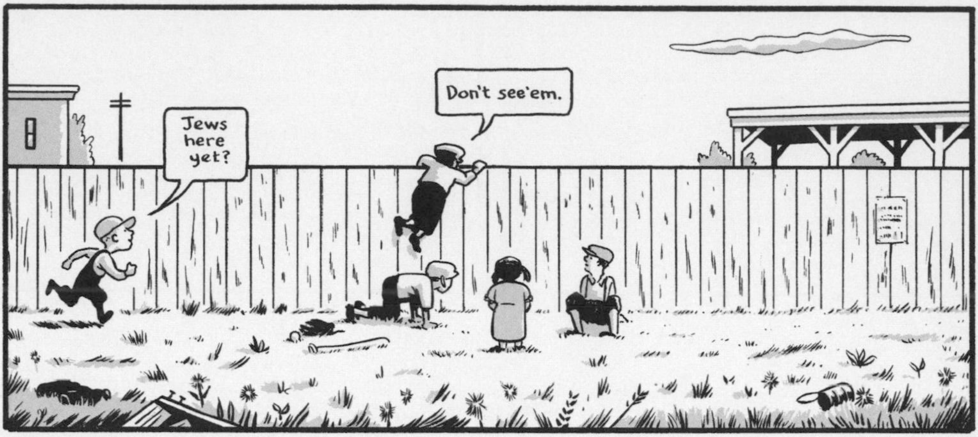
Jews here yet?
Don't see'em.

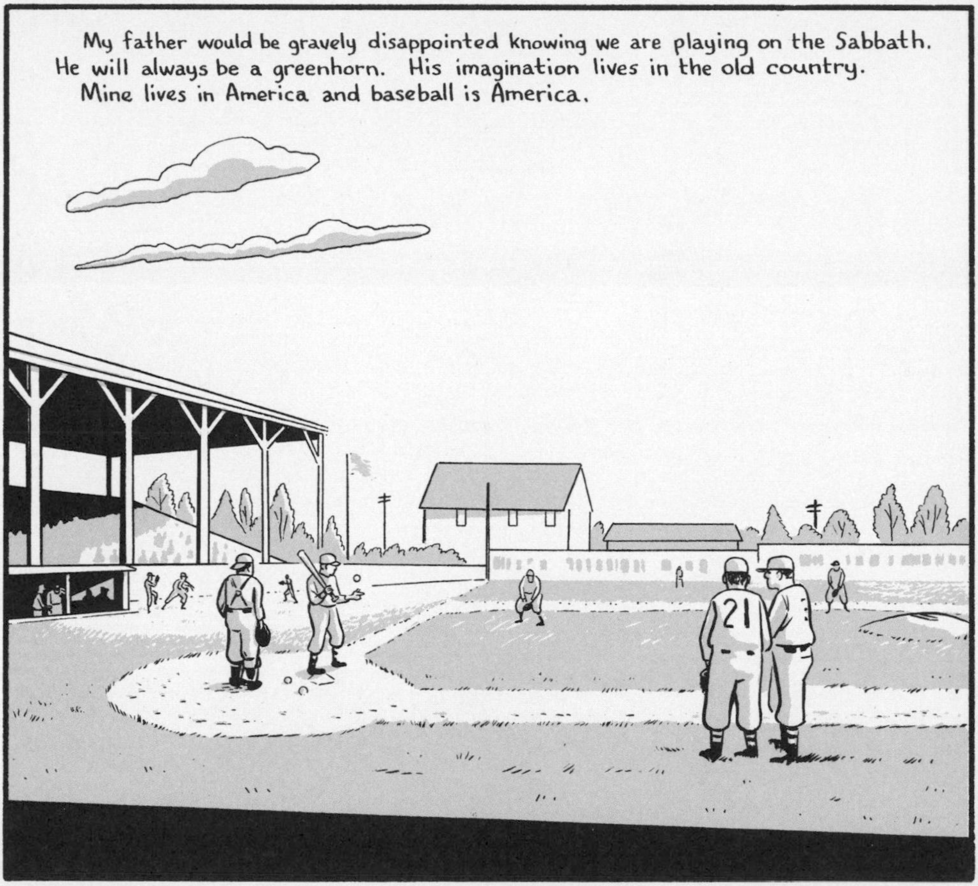
My father would be gravely disappointed knowing we are playing on the Sabbath. He will always be a greenhorn. His imagination lives in the old country.
Mine lives in America and baseball is America.
21

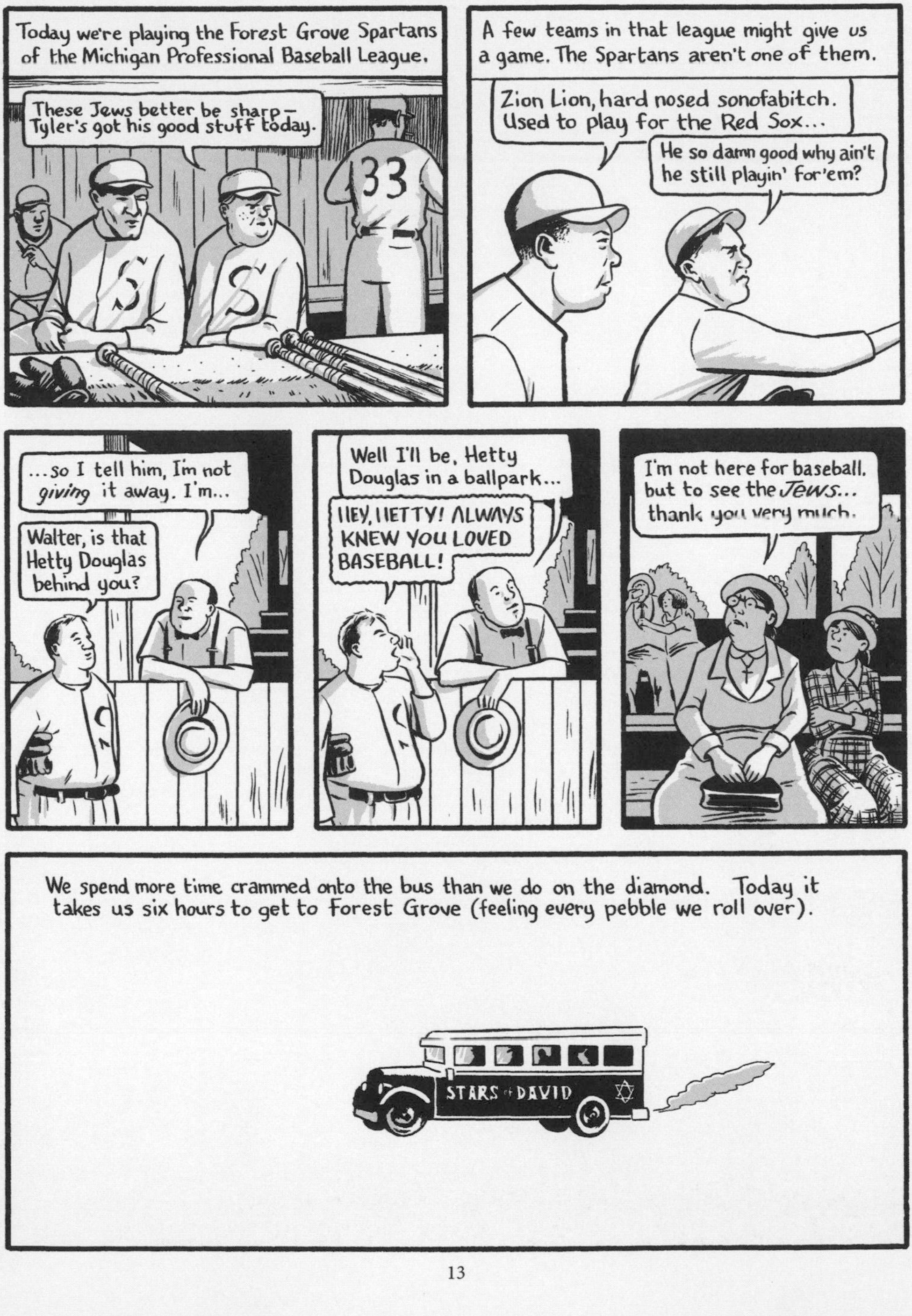
Today we're playing the Forest Grove Spartans of the Michigan Professional Baseball League.
These Jews better be sharp— Tyler's got his good stuff today.
33
A few teams in that league might give us a game. The Spartans aren't one of them.
Zion Lion, hard nosed sonofabitch. Used to play for the Red Sox...
He so damn good why ain't he still playin' for'em?
...so I tell him, I'm not *giving* it away. I'm...
Walter, is that Hetty Douglas behind you?
Well I'll be, Hetty Douglas in a ballpark...
HEY, HETTY! ALWAYS KNEW YOU LOVED BASEBALL!
I'm not here for baseball, but to see the *JEWS*... thank you very much.
We spend more time crammed onto the bus than we do on the diamond. Today it takes us six hours to get to Forest Grove (feeling every pebble we roll over).
STARS of DAVID

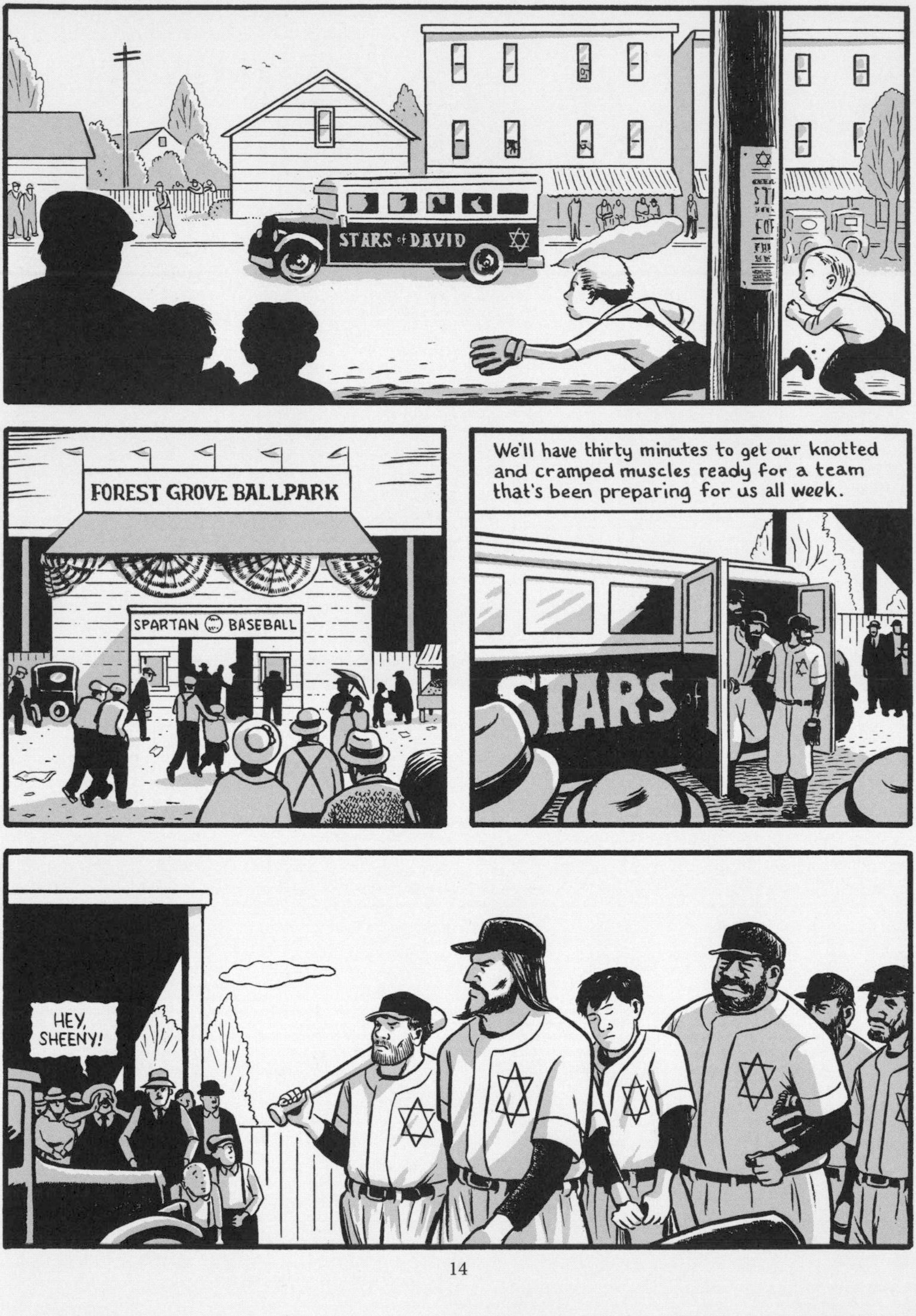
STARS of DAVID
FOREST GROVE BALLPARK
SPARTAN BASEBALL
We'll have thirty minutes to get our knotted and cramped muscles ready for a team that's been preparing for us all week.
STARS
HEY, SHEENY!

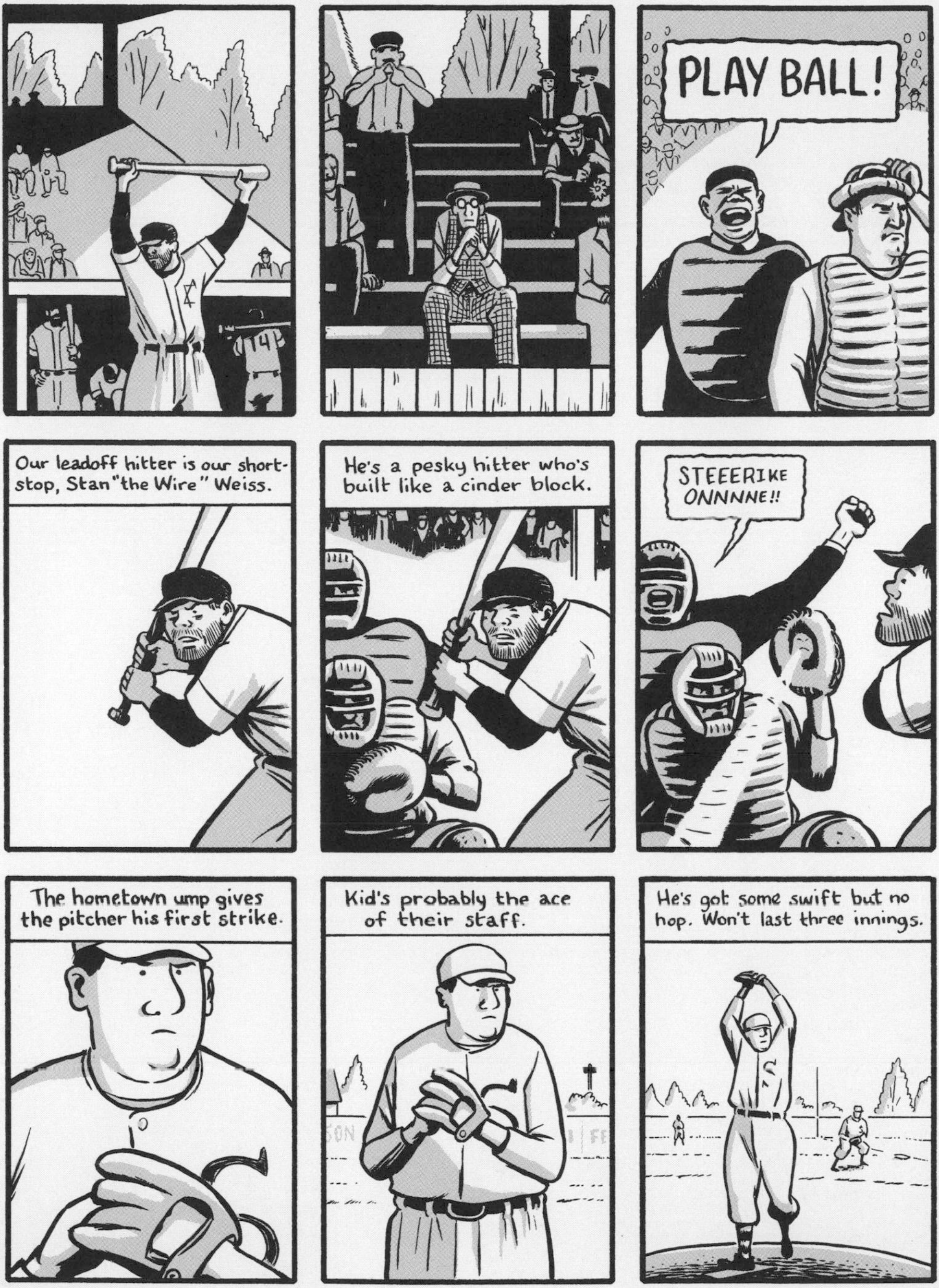
PLAY BALL!
Our leadoff hitter is our short-stop, Stan "the Wire" Weiss.
He's a pesky hitter who's built like a cinder block.
STEEERIKE ONNNNE!!
The hometown ump gives the pitcher his first strike.
Kid's probably the ace of their staff.
He's got some swift but no hop. Won't last three innings.

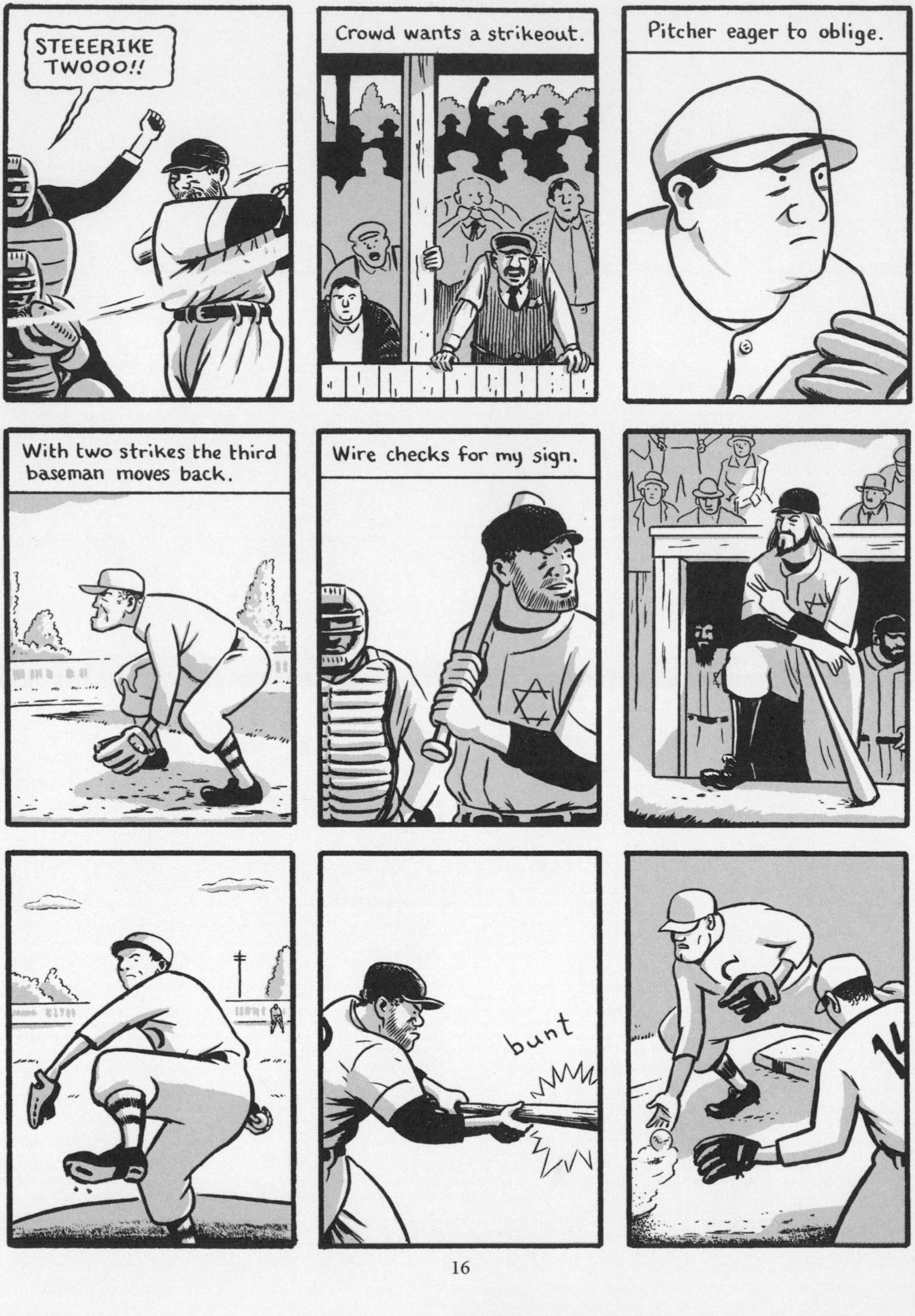
STEEERIKE TWOOO!!
Crowd wants a strikeout.
Pitcher eager to oblige.
With two strikes the third baseman moves back.
Wire checks for my sign.
bunt

Not even a throw.

One on, no out.

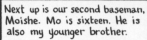

Next up is our second baseman, Moishe. Mo is sixteen. He is also my younger brother.

Time out, Fred.

TIME OUT!

The Jew at the plate is just a kid. That's not a beard, it's shoe polish.

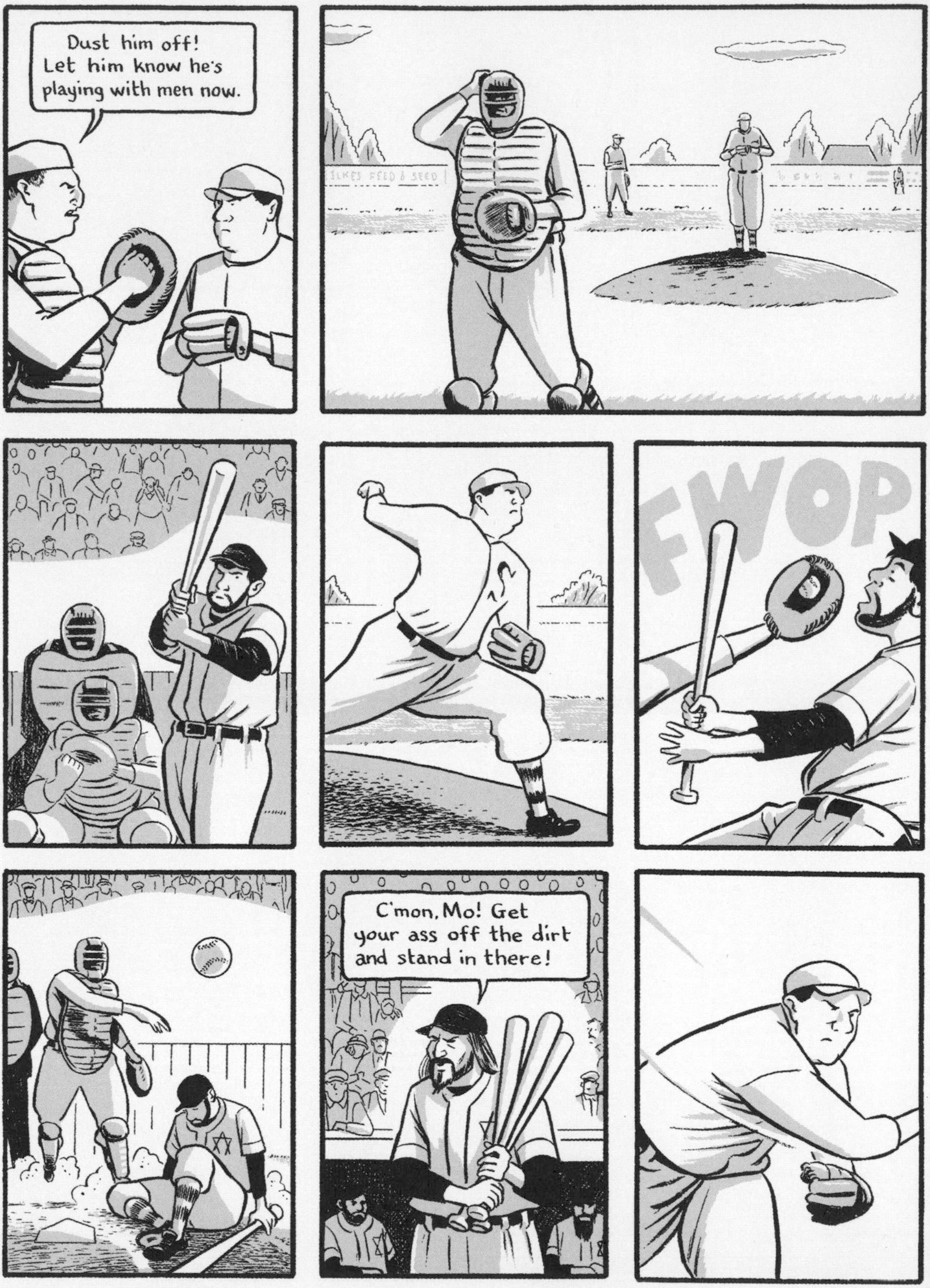
Dust him off! Let him know he's playing with men now.
FWOP
C'mon, Mo! Get your ass off the dirt and stand in there!

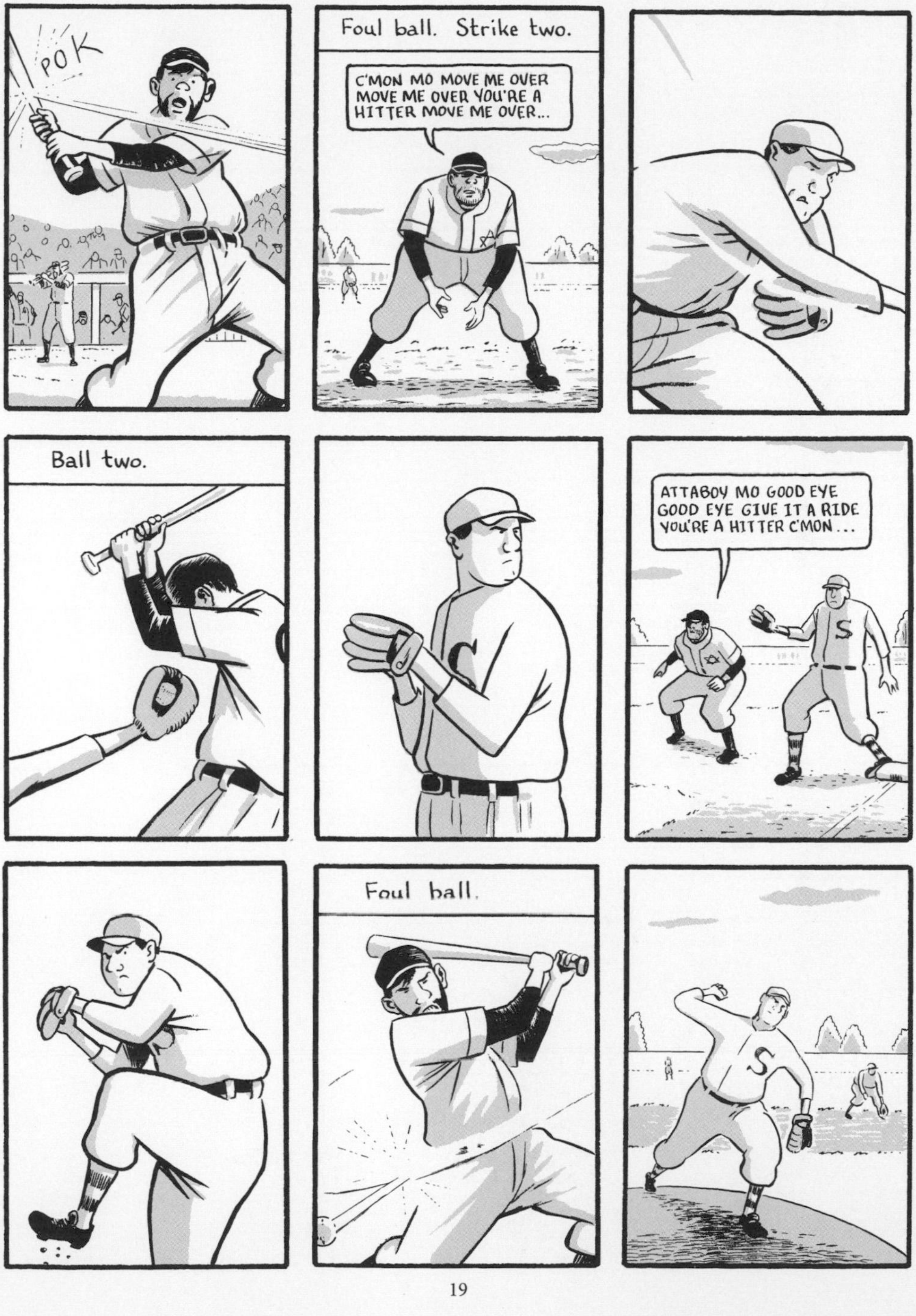
POK
Foul ball. Strike two.
C'MON MO MOVE ME OVER MOVE ME OVER YOU'RE A HITTER MOVE ME OVER...
Ball two.
ATTABOY MO GOOD EYE GOOD EYE GIVE IT A RIDE YOU'RE A HITTER C'MON...
Foul ball.

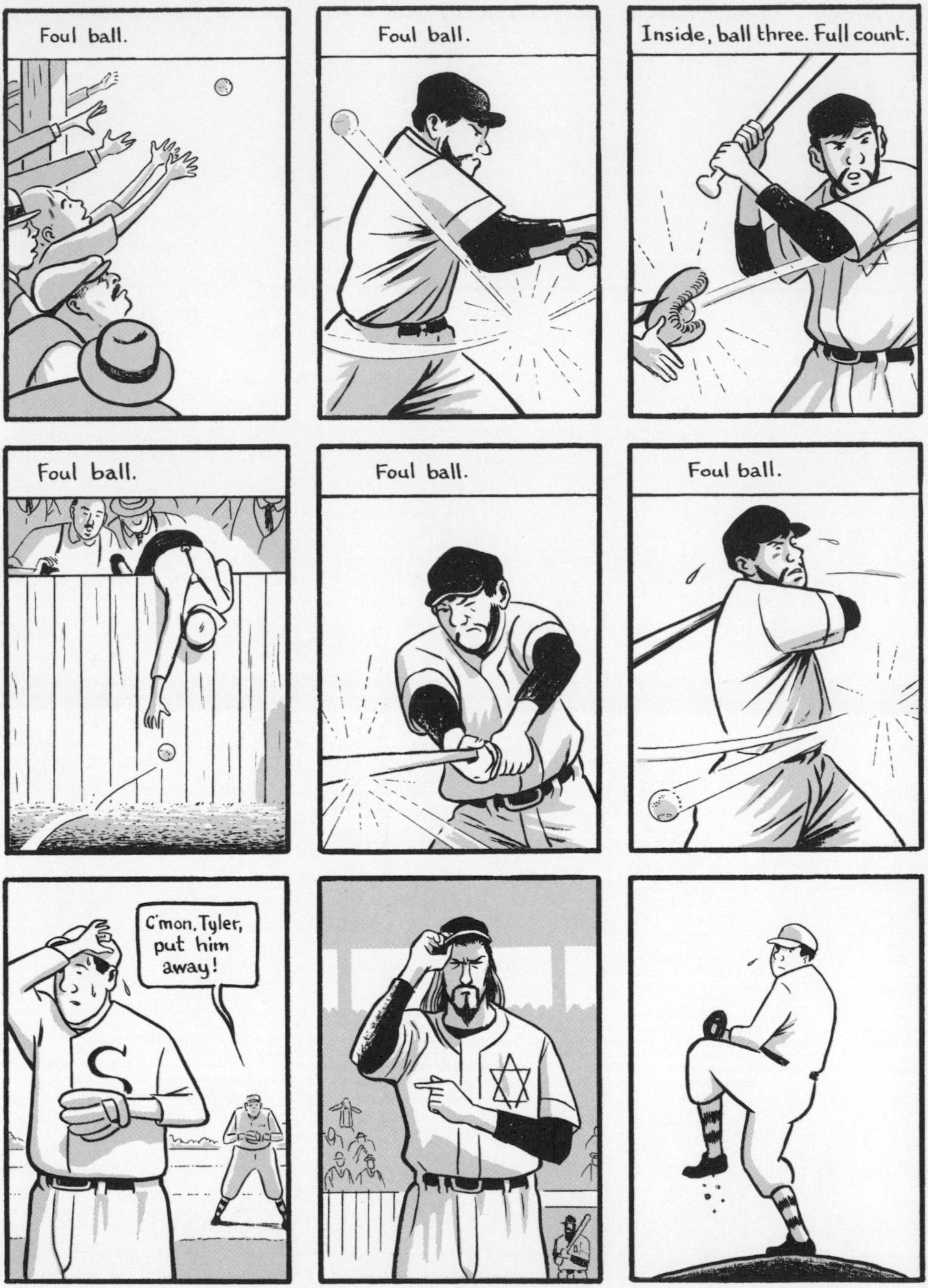
Foul ball.
Foul ball.
Inside, ball three. Full count.
Foul ball.
Foul ball.
Foul ball.
C'mon, Tyler, put him away!

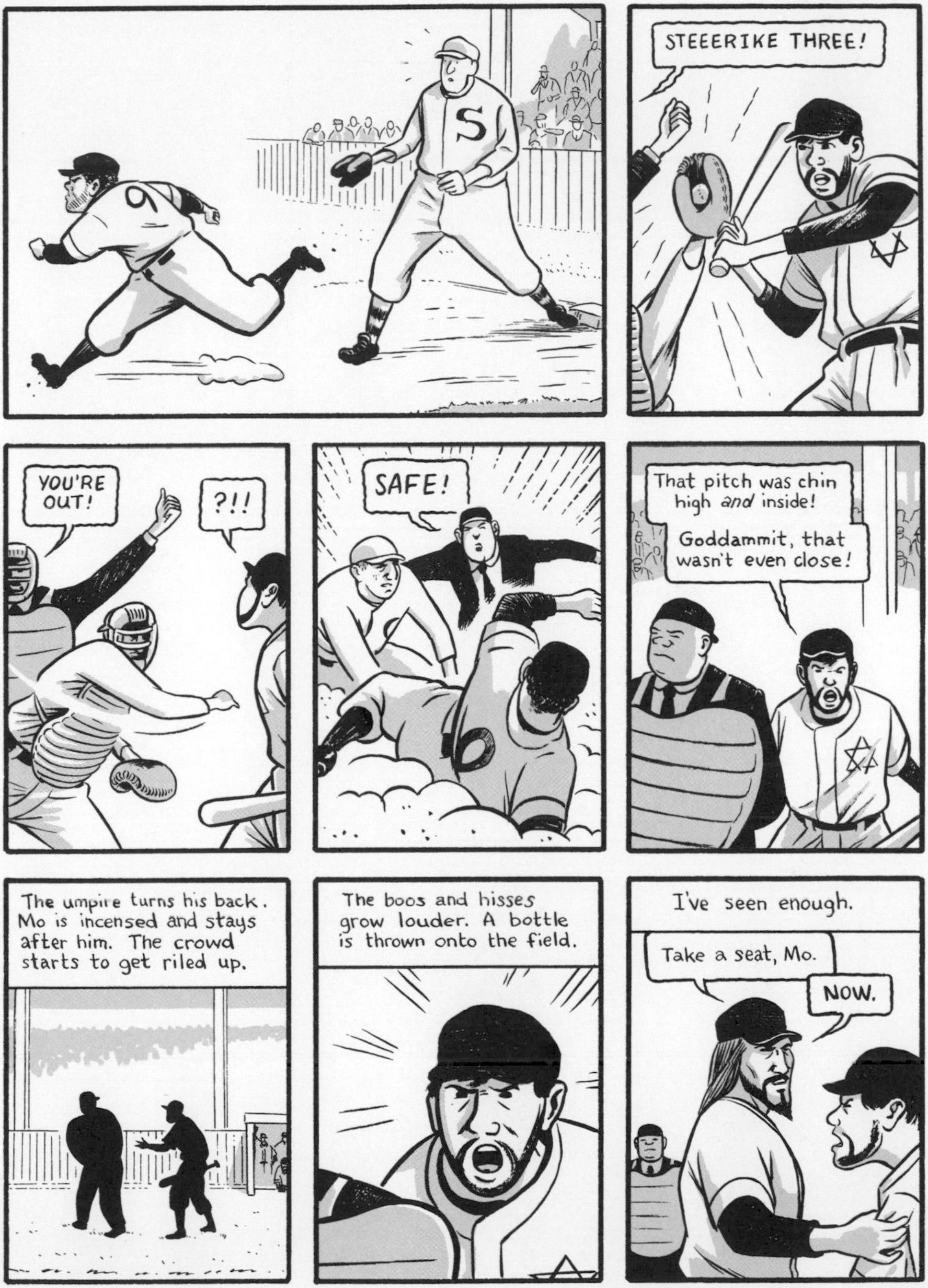
STEEERIKE THREE!
YOU'RE OUT!
?!!
SAFE!
That pitch was chin high *and* inside!
Goddammit, that wasn't even close!
The umpire turns his back. Mo is incensed and stays after him. The crowd starts to get riled up.
The boos and hisses grow louder. A bottle is thrown onto the field.
I've seen enough.
Take a seat, Mo.
NOW.

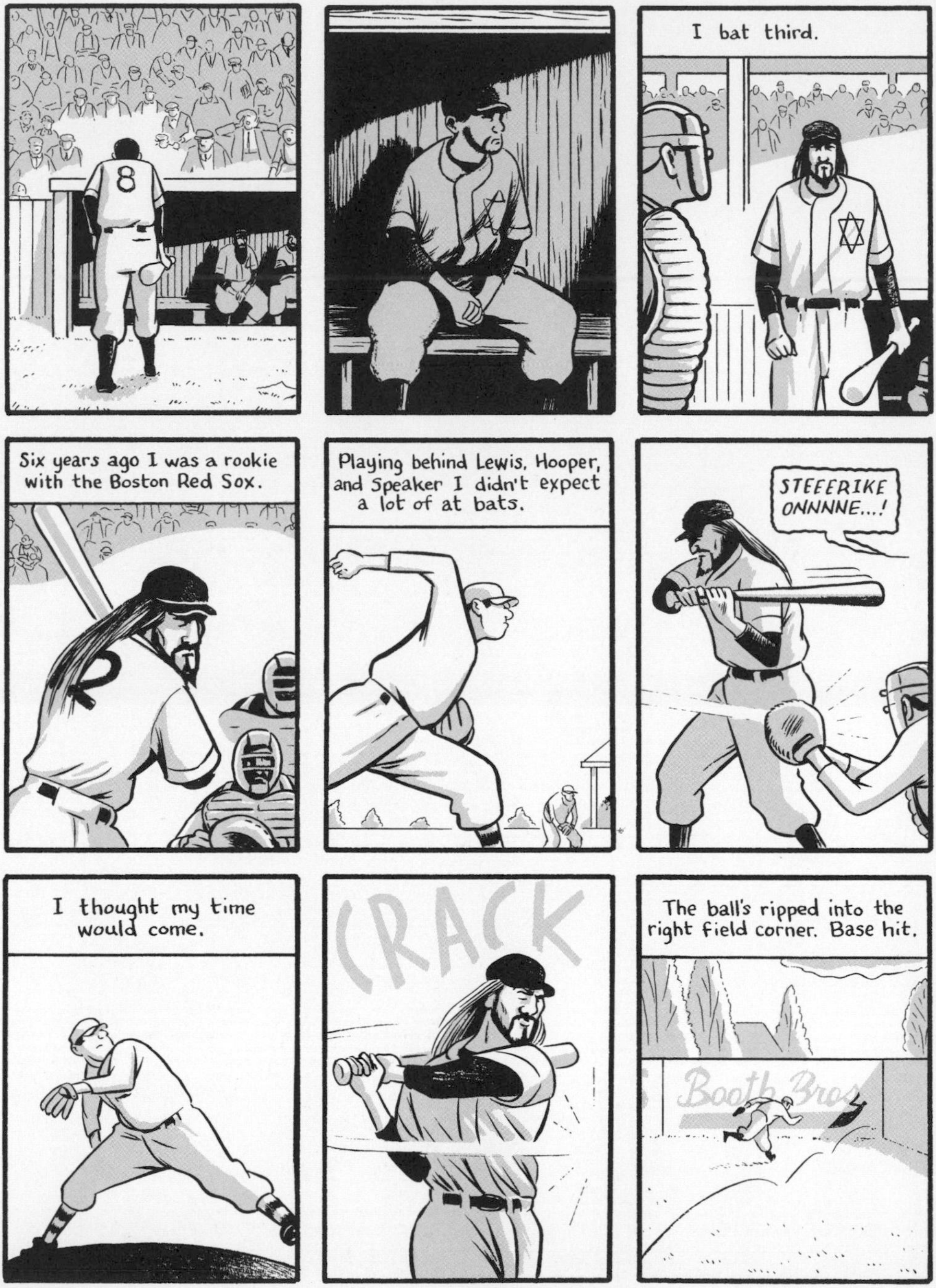

I bat third.
Six years ago I was a rookie with the Boston Red Sox.
Playing behind Lewis, Hooper, and Speaker I didn't expect a lot of at bats.
STEEERIKE ONNNNE...!
I thought my time would come.
CRACK
The ball's ripped into the right field corner. Base hit.
Booth Bros

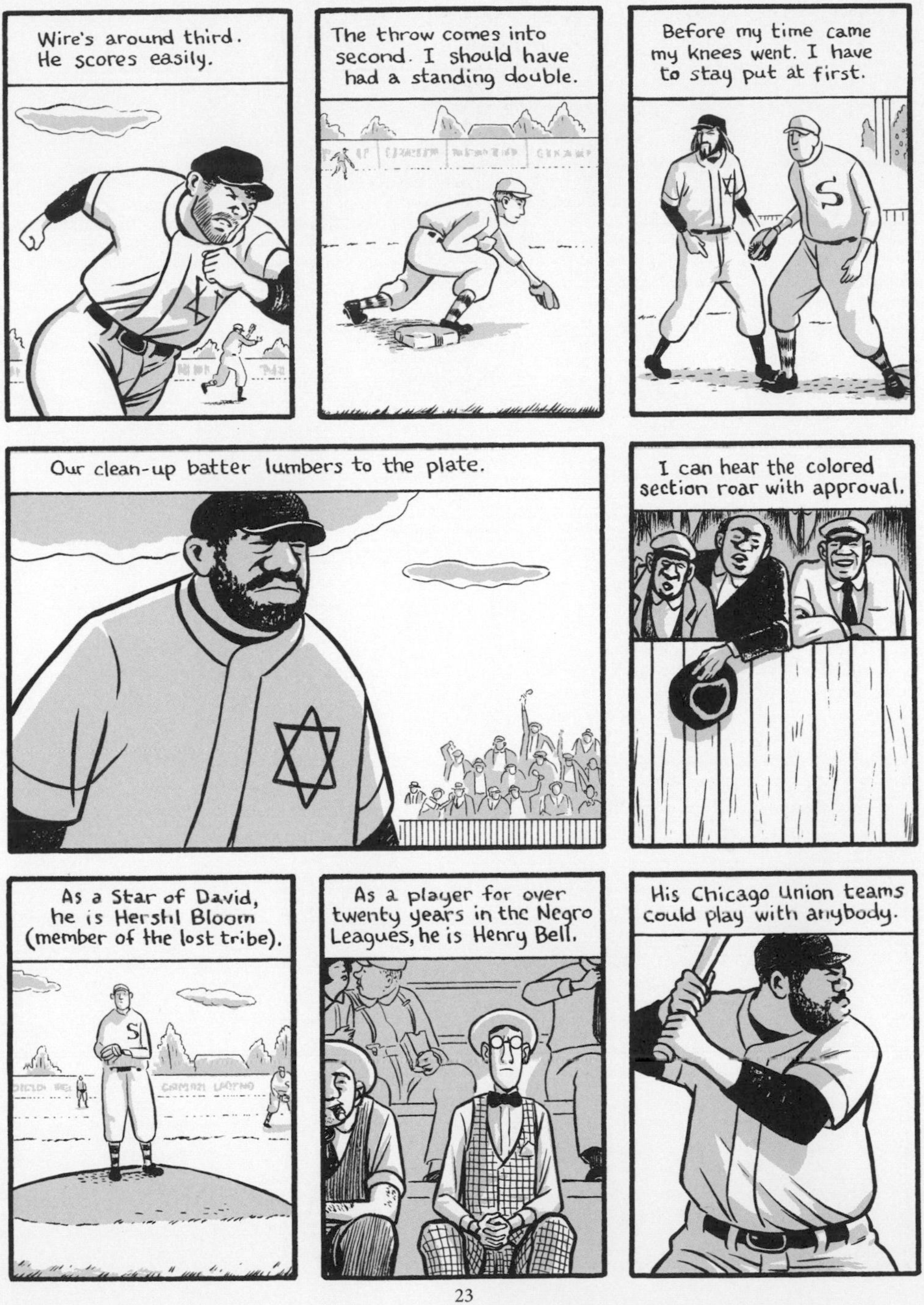
Wire's around third. He scores easily.
The throw comes into second. I should have had a standing double.
Before my time came my knees went. I have to stay put at first.
Our clean-up batter lumbers to the plate.
I can hear the colored section roar with approval.
As a Star of David, he is Hershl Bloom (member of the lost tribe).
As a player for over twenty years in the Negro Leagues, he is Henry Bell.
His Chicago Union teams could play with anybody.

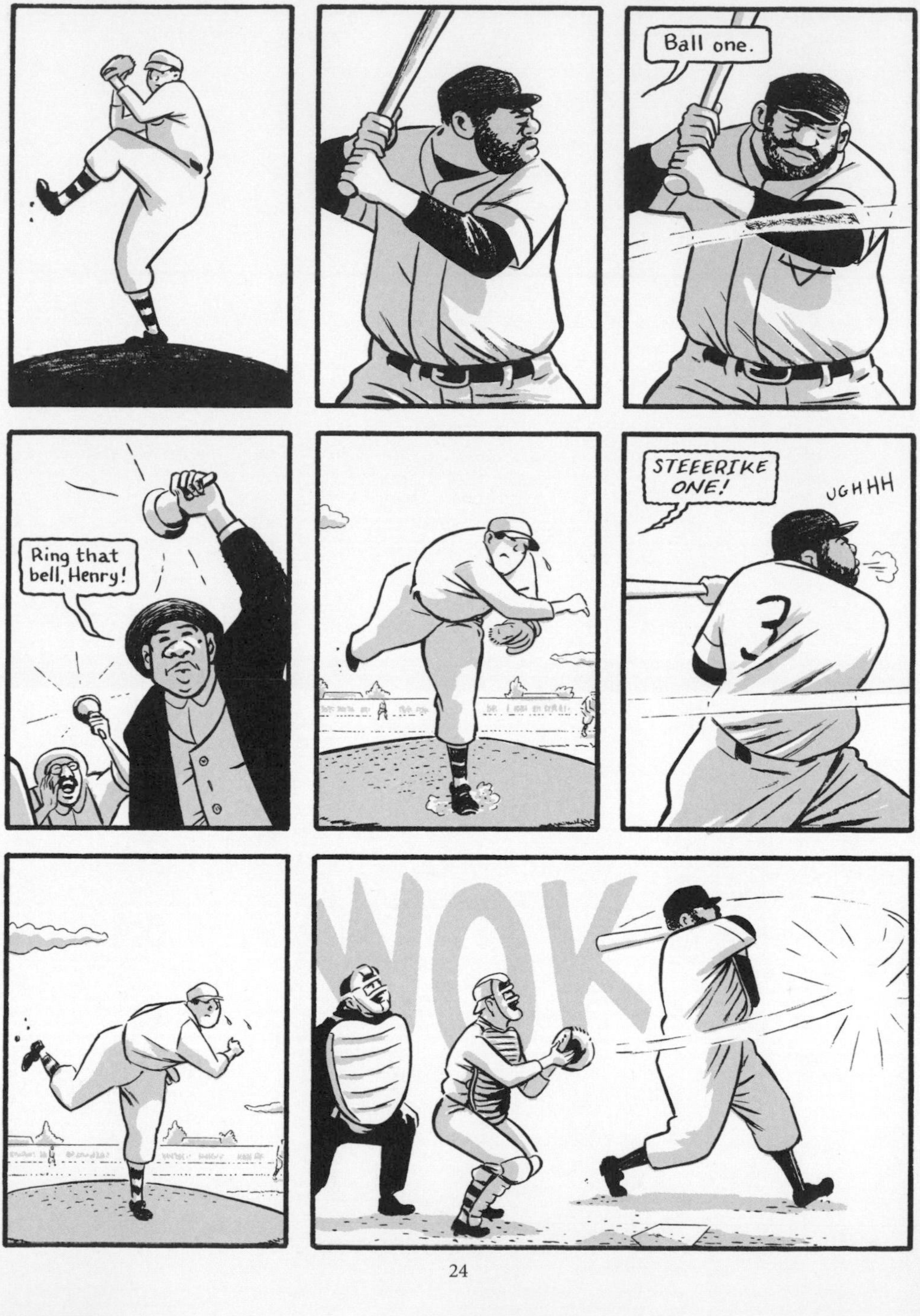
Ball one.
Ring that bell, Henry!
STEEERIKE ONE!
UGHHH
WOK

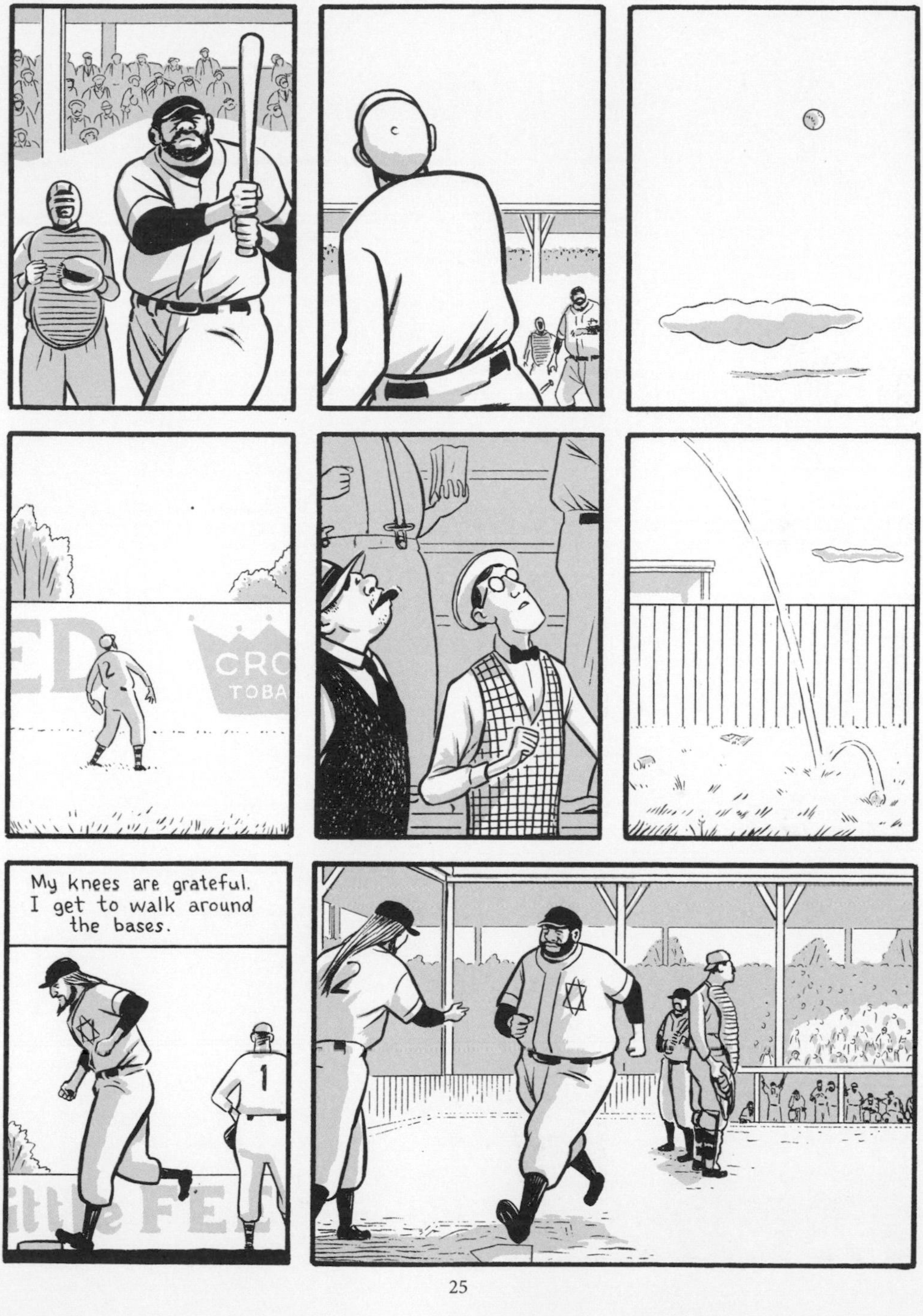
ED
CRO
TOBA
My knees are grateful. I get to walk around the bases.
1
ittle FE
2

The rest of the game is sloppy as we play down to the level of our opponent. Mo's error in the fourth costs us two runs.

| VISITORS | 4 | 2 | 1 | 0 | 2 | 0 | 1 | 0 | | | 10 |
| SPARTANS | 0 | 0 | 1 | 3 | 0 | 0 | 1 | 2 | | | 7 |

Bottom of the eighth: Forest Grove continues to put runs on the board. Another single, another run in.

The crowd rises to its feet, rallying their team.

My pitcher, Buttercup Lev, is throwing on only two days rest. He's already thrown 130 pitches.

Buttercup is a slowball pitcher, so even when fresh he's not going to overwhelm anyone.

He hits the corners and changes speed (slow and slower).

You could count the stitches on the ball as it crosses the plate.

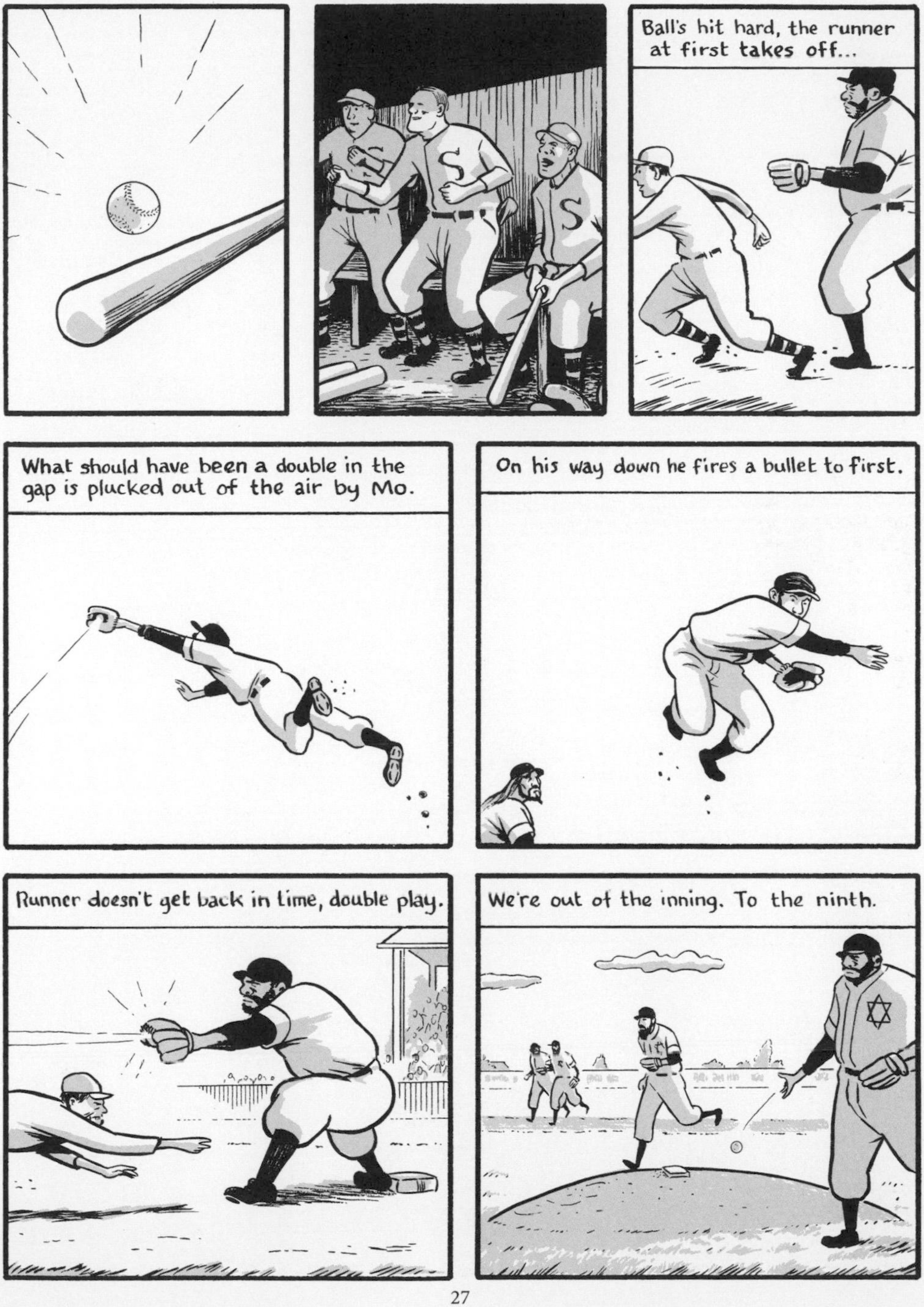
Ball's hit hard, the runner at first takes off...
What should have been a double in the gap is plucked out of the air by Mo.
On his way down he fires a bullet to first.
Runner doesn't get back in time, double play.
We're out of the inning. To the ninth.

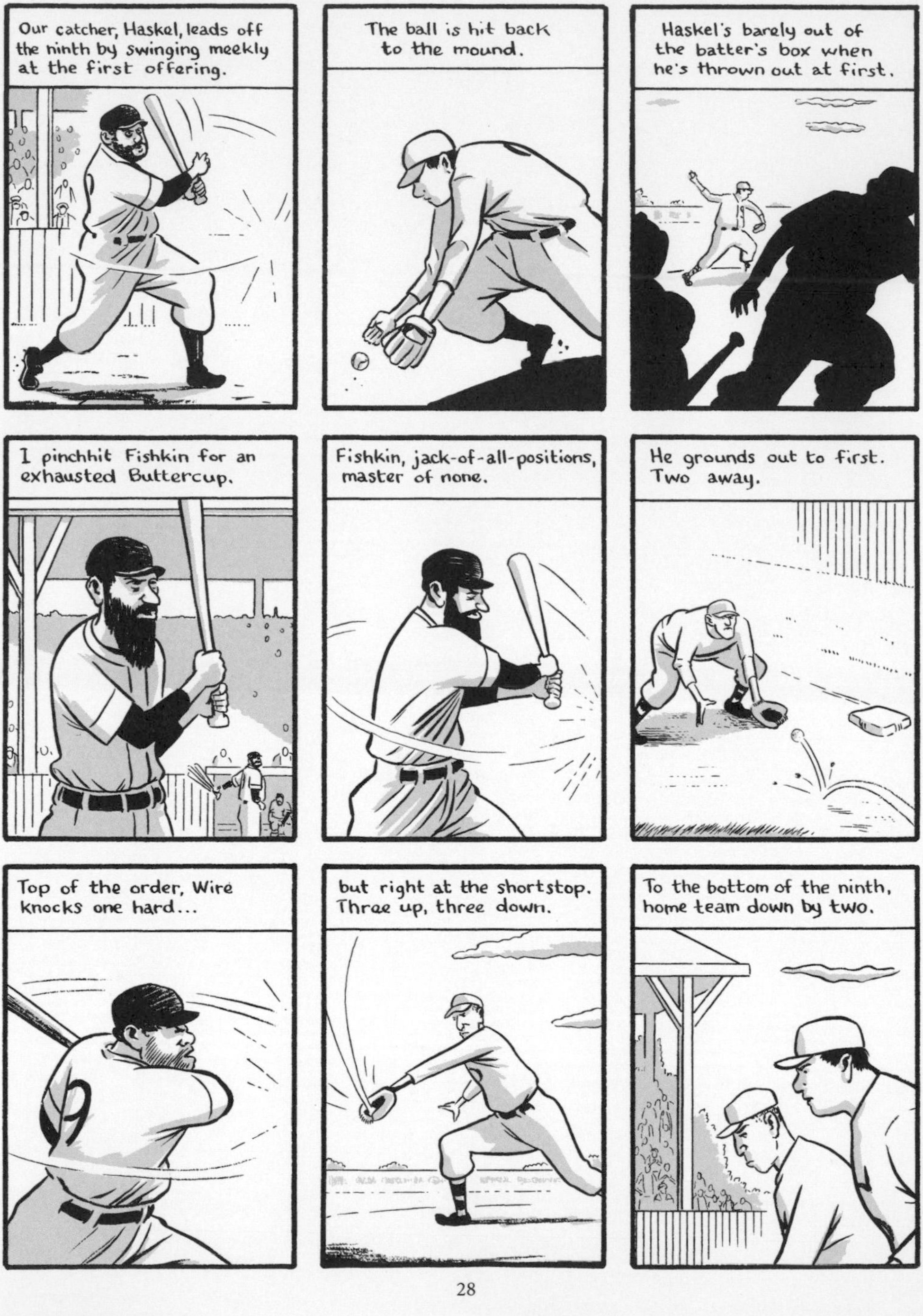
Our catcher, Haskel, leads off the ninth by swinging meekly at the first offering.
The ball is hit back to the mound.
Haskel's barely out of the batter's box when he's thrown out at first.
I pinchhit Fishkin for an exhausted Buttercup.
Fishkin, jack-of-all-positions, master of none.
He grounds out to first. Two away.
Top of the order, Wire knocks one hard...
but right at the shortstop. Three up, three down.
To the bottom of the ninth, home team down by two.

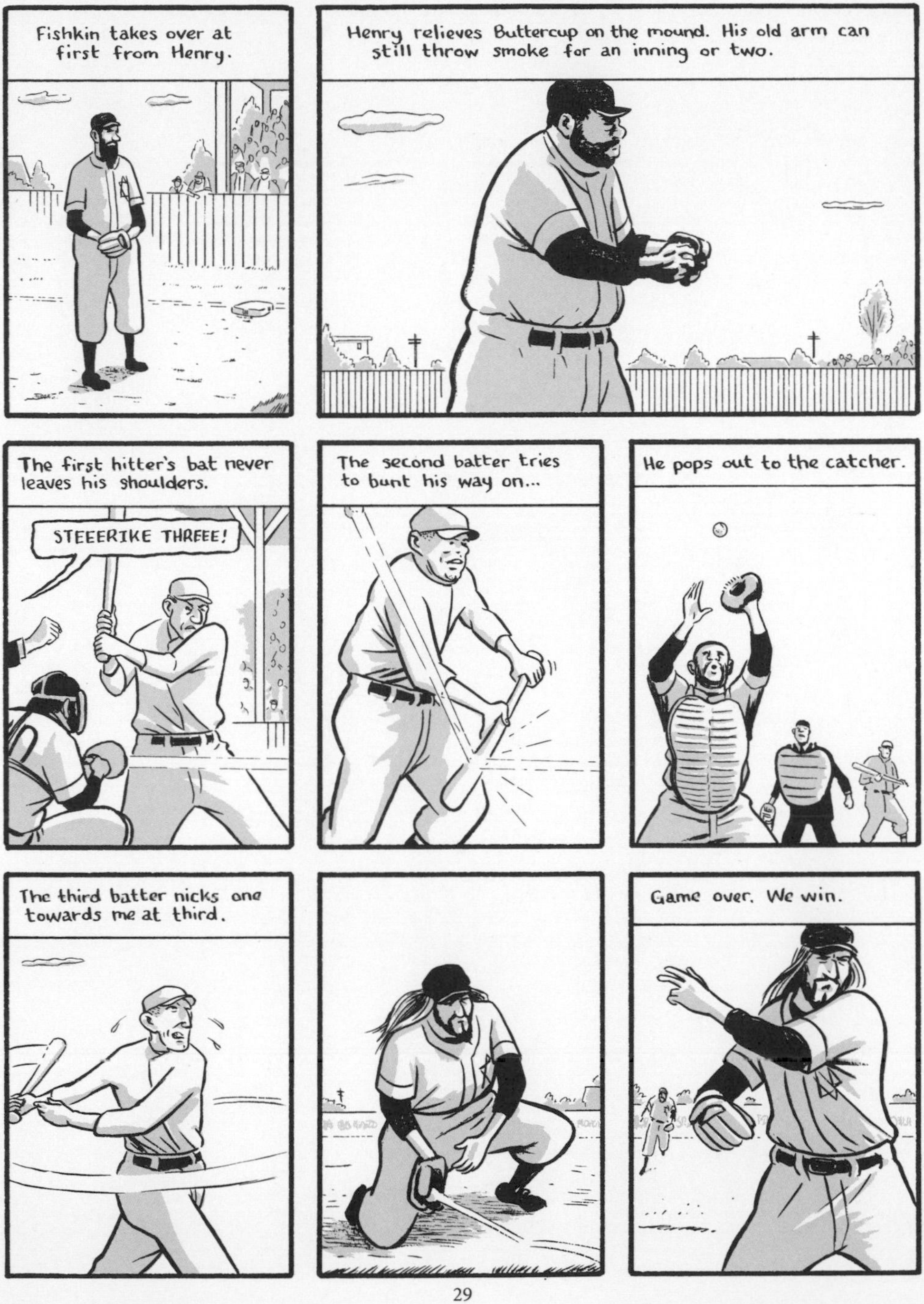

Fishkin takes over at first from Henry.
Henry relieves Buttercup on the mound. His old arm can still throw smoke for an inning or two.
The first hitter's bat never leaves his shoulders.
STEEERIKE THREEE!
The second batter tries to bunt his way on...
He pops out to the catcher.
The third batter nicks one towards me at third.
Game over. We win.

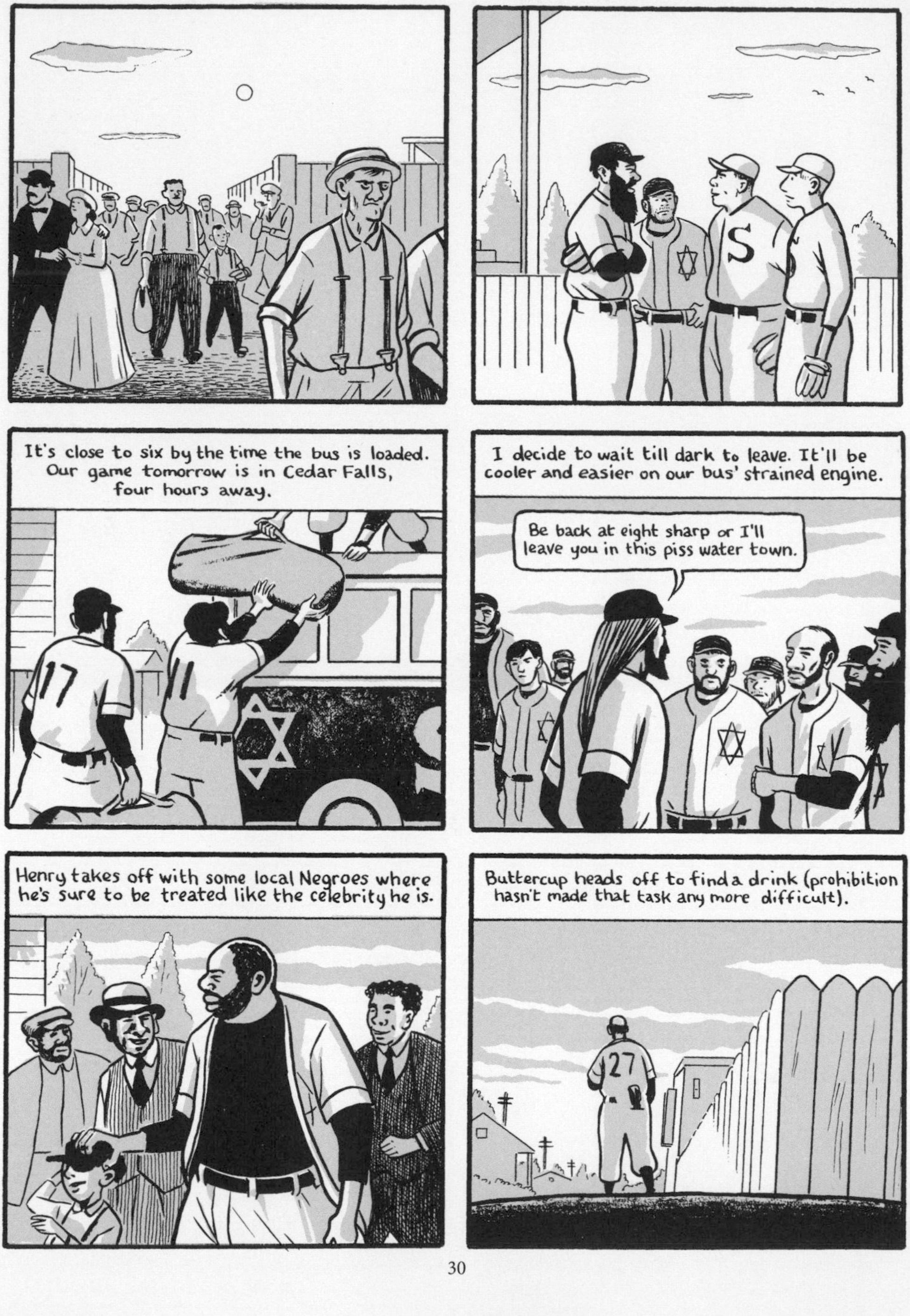
It's close to six by the time the bus is loaded. Our game tomorrow is in Cedar Falls, four hours away.
I decide to wait till dark to leave. It'll be cooler and easier on our bus' strained engine.
Be back at eight sharp or I'll leave you in this piss water town.
17
11
Henry takes off with some local Negroes where he's sure to be treated like the celebrity he is.
Buttercup heads off to find a drink (prohibition hasn't made that task any more difficult).
27

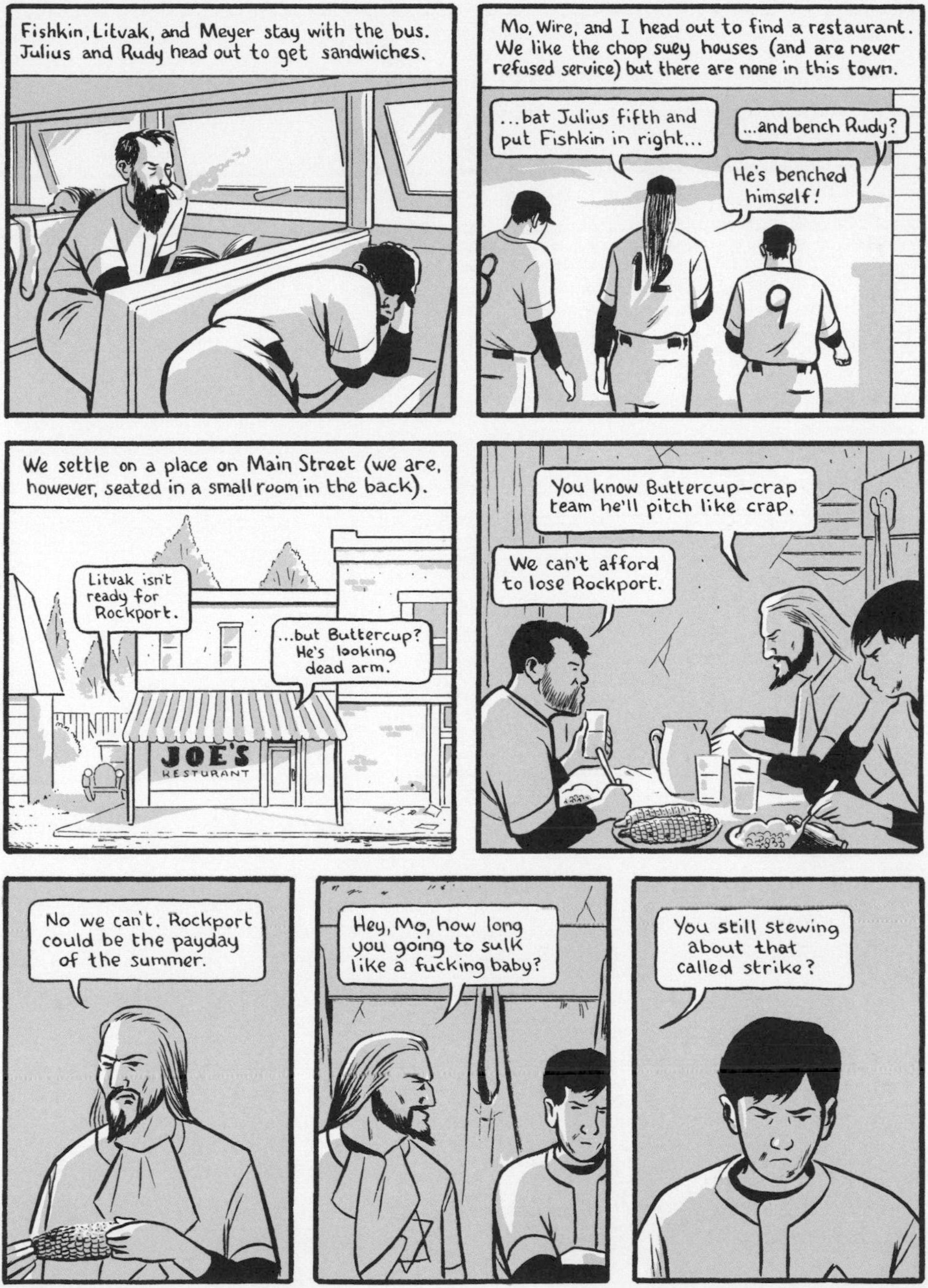
Fishkin, Litvak, and Meyer stay with the bus. Julius and Rudy head out to get sandwiches.
Mo, Wire, and I head out to find a restaurant. We like the chop suey houses (and are never refused service) but there are none in this town.
...bat Julius fifth and put Fishkin in right...
...and bench Rudy?
He's benched himself!
We settle on a place on Main Street (we are, however, seated in a small room in the back).
Litvak isn't ready for Rockport.
...but Buttercup? He's looking dead arm.
JOE'S
RESTURANT
You know Buttercup—crap team he'll pitch like crap.
We can't afford to lose Rockport.
No we can't. Rockport could be the payday of the summer.
Hey, Mo, how long you going to sulk like a fucking baby?
You still stewing about that called strike?

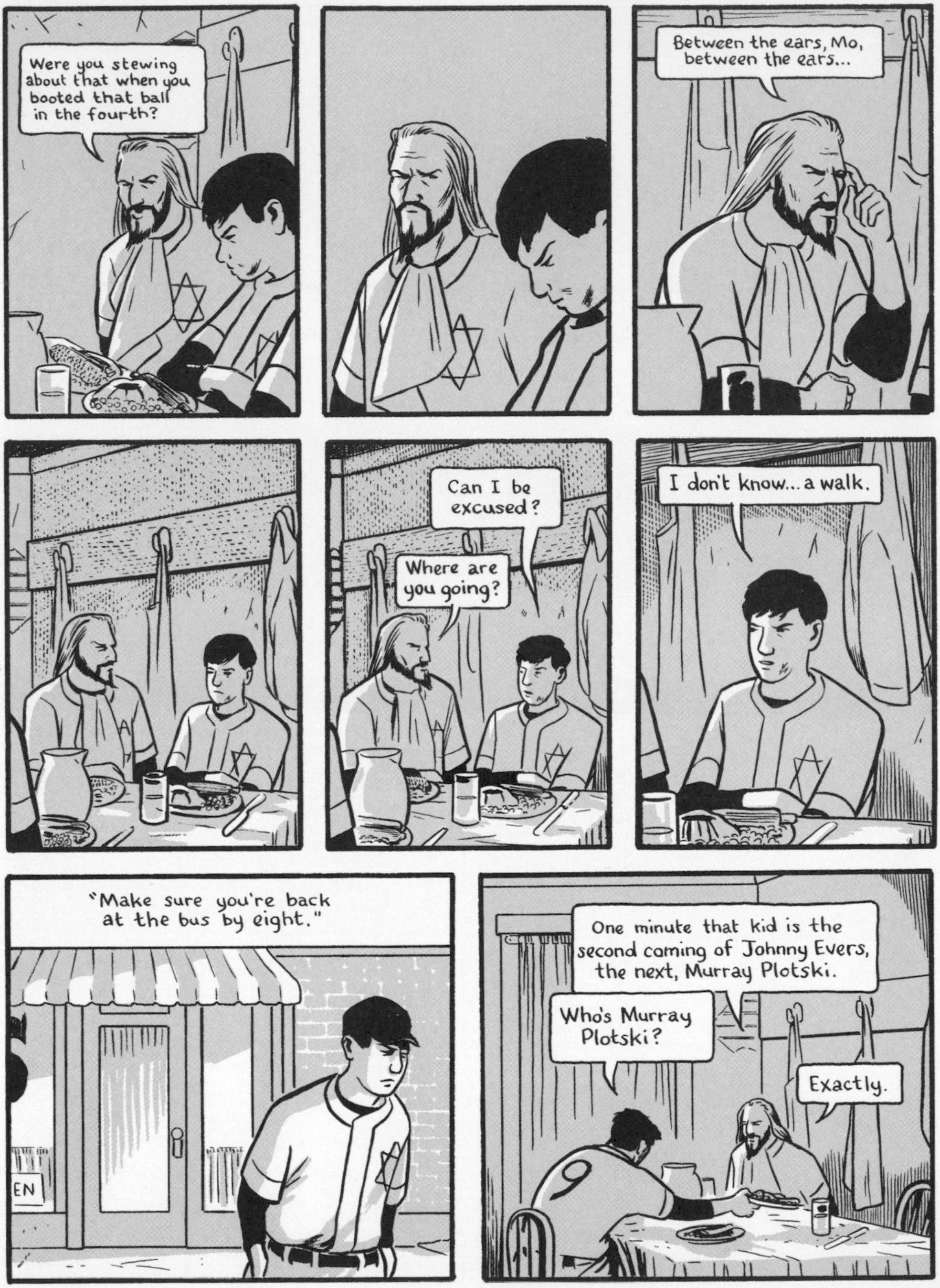
Were you stewing about that when you booted that ball in the fourth?
Between the ears, Mo, between the ears...
Can I be excused?
Where are you going?
I don't know... a walk.
"Make sure you're back at the bus by eight."
EN
One minute that kid is the second coming of Johnny Evers, the next, Murray Plotski.
Who's Murray Plotski?
Exactly.

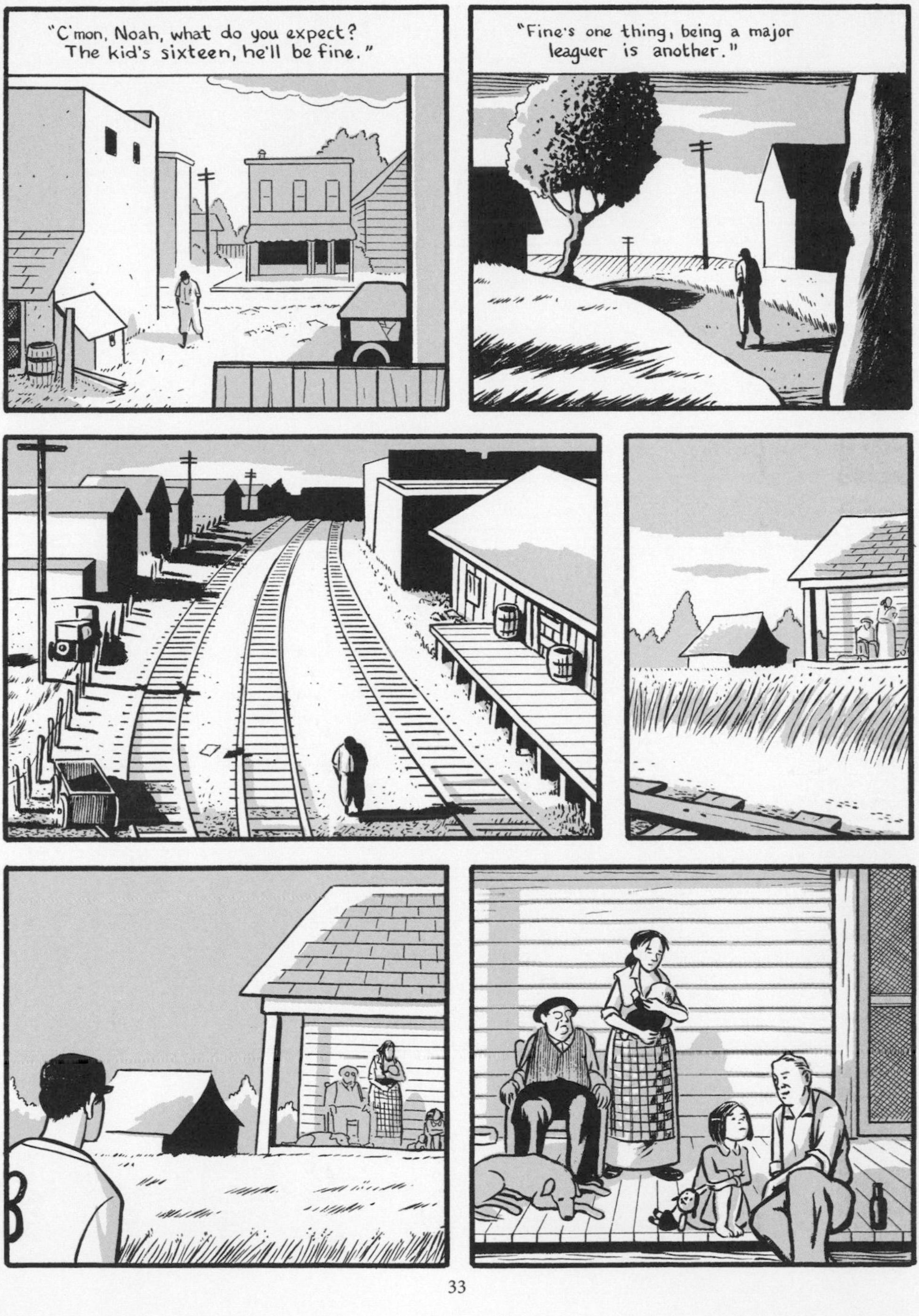
"C'mon, Noah, what do you expect? The kid's sixteen, he'll be fine."
"Fine's one thing, being a major leaguer is another."

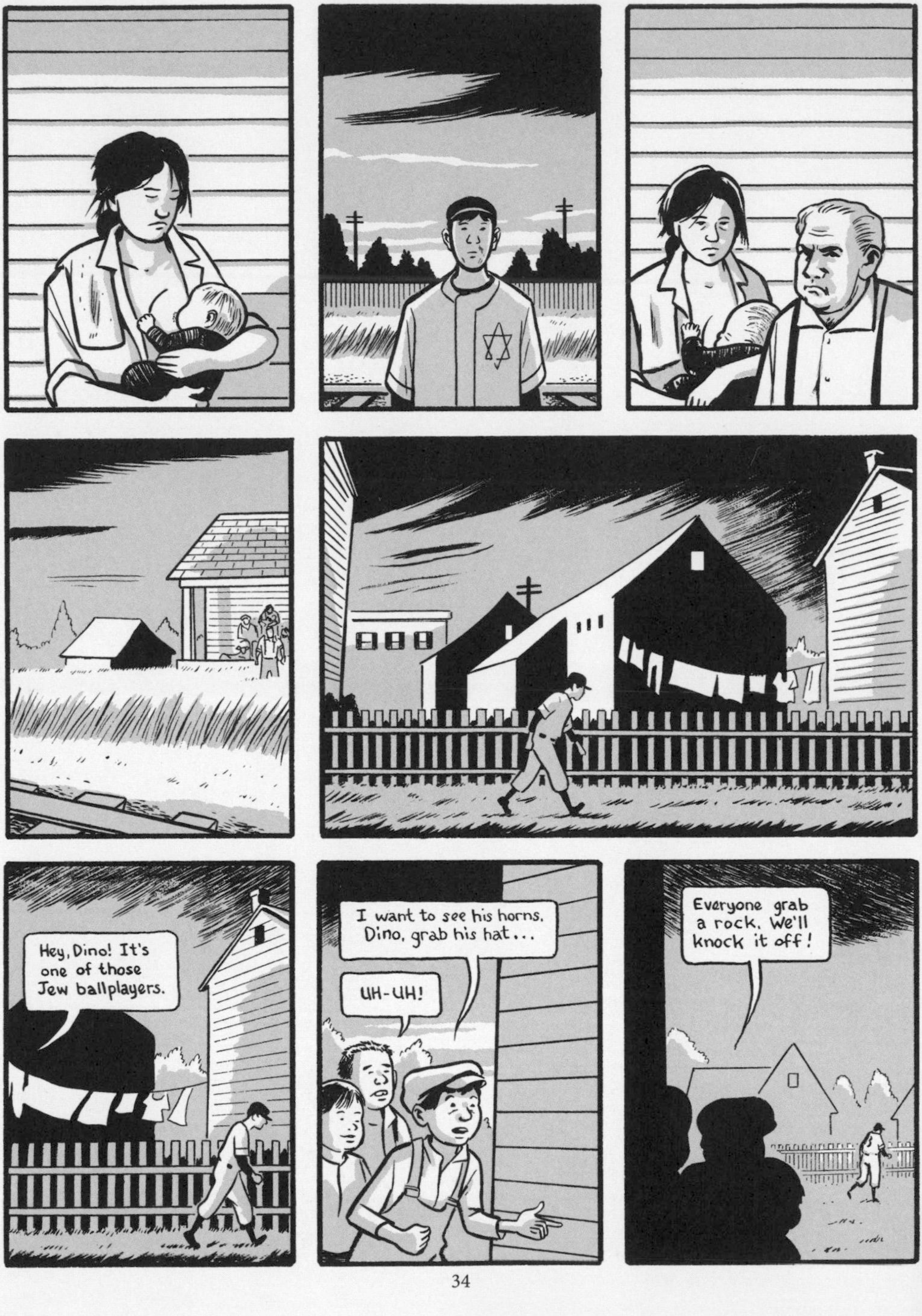

Hey, Dino! It's one of those Jew ballplayers.
I want to see his horns. Dino, grab his hat...
UH-UH!
Everyone grab a rock. We'll knock it off!

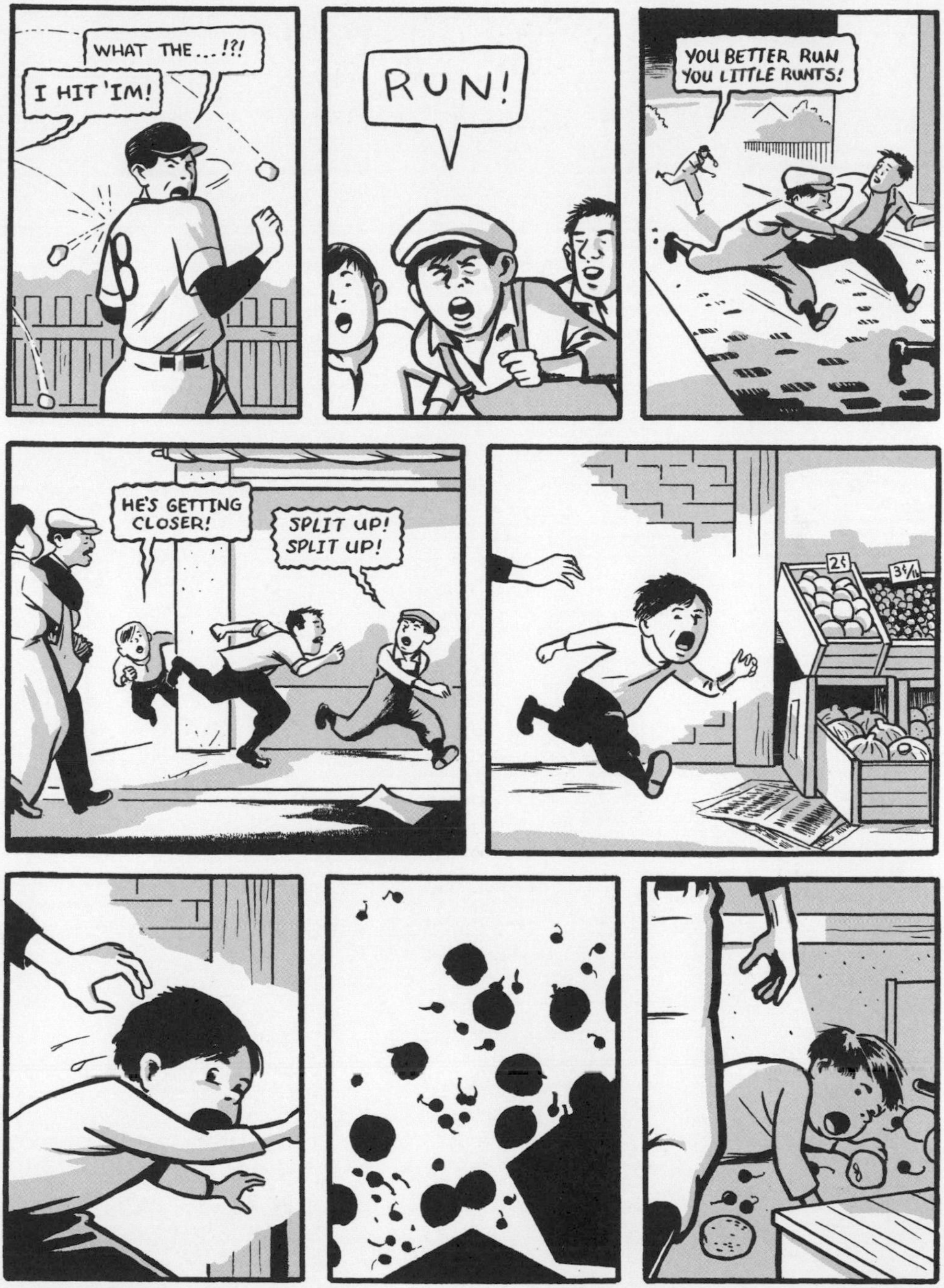
WHAT THE ...!?!
I HIT 'IM!
RUN!
YOU BETTER RUN YOU LITTLE RUNTS!
HE'S GETTING CLOSER!
SPLIT UP! SPLIT UP!
2¢
3¢/lb

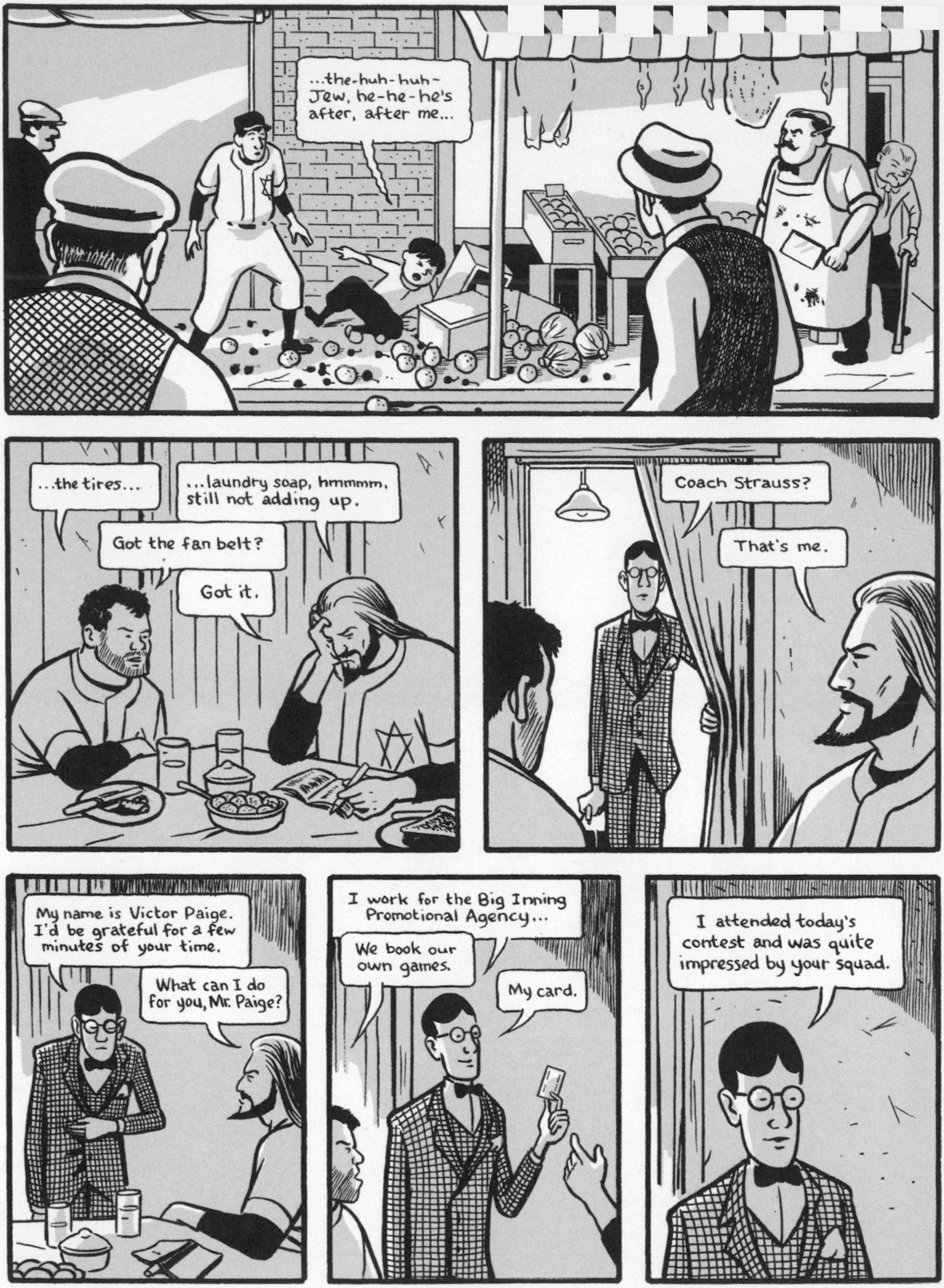
...the-huh-huh-Jew, he-he-he's after, after me...
...the tires...
...laundry soap, hmmmm, still not adding up.
Got the fan belt?
Got it.
Coach Strauss?
That's me.
My name is Victor Paige. I'd be grateful for a few minutes of your time.
What can I do for you, Mr. Paige?
I work for the Big Inning Promotional Agency...
We book our own games.
My card.
I attended today's contest and was quite impressed by your squad.

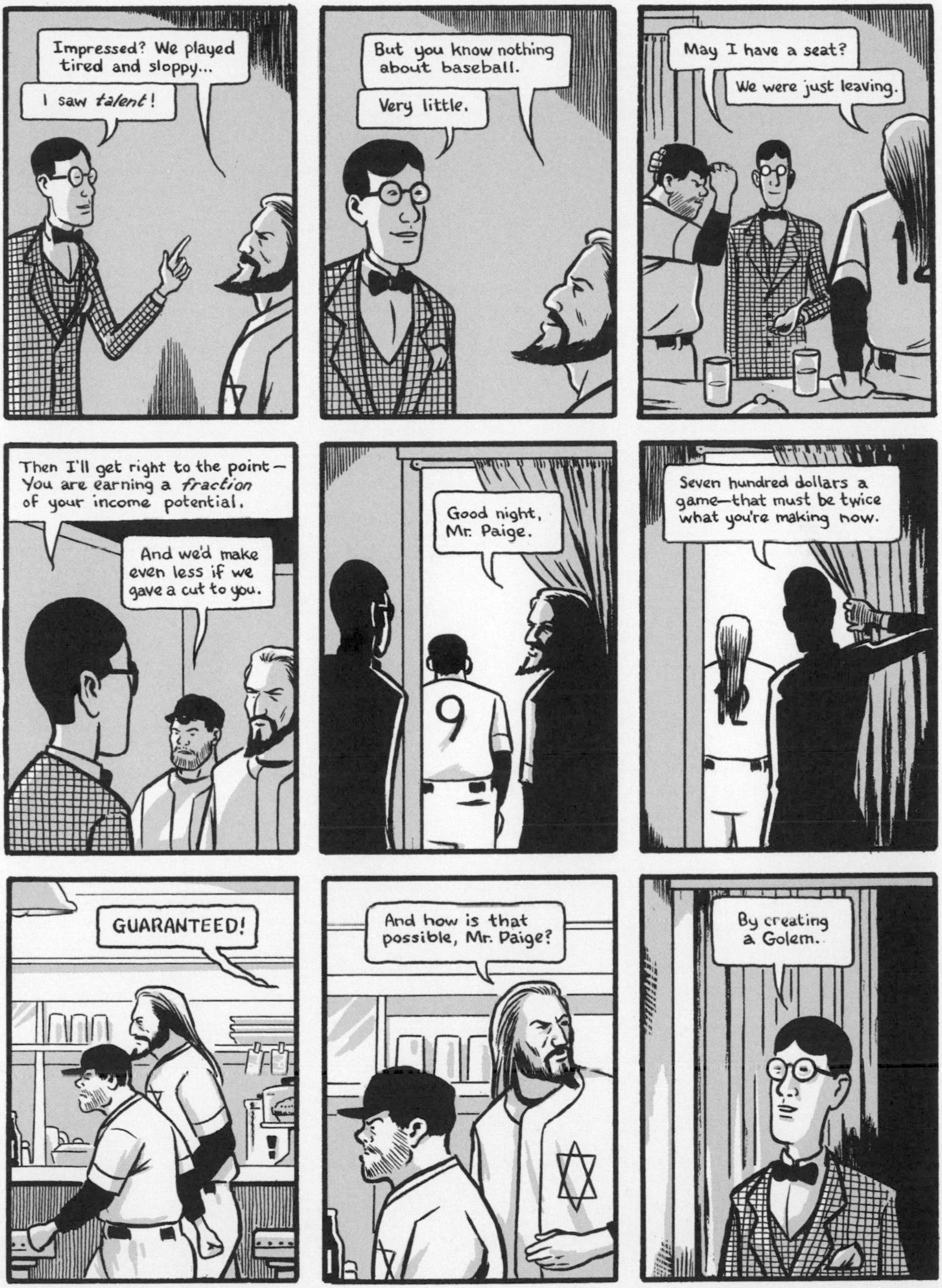
Impressed? We played tired and sloppy...
I saw *talent*!
But you know nothing about baseball.
Very little.
May I have a seat?
We were just leaving.
Then I'll get right to the point— You are earning a *fraction* of your income potential.
And we'd make even less if we gave a cut to you.
Good night, Mr. Paige.
Seven hundred dollars a game—that must be twice what you're making now.
GUARANTEED!
And how is that possible, Mr. Paige?
By creating a Golem.

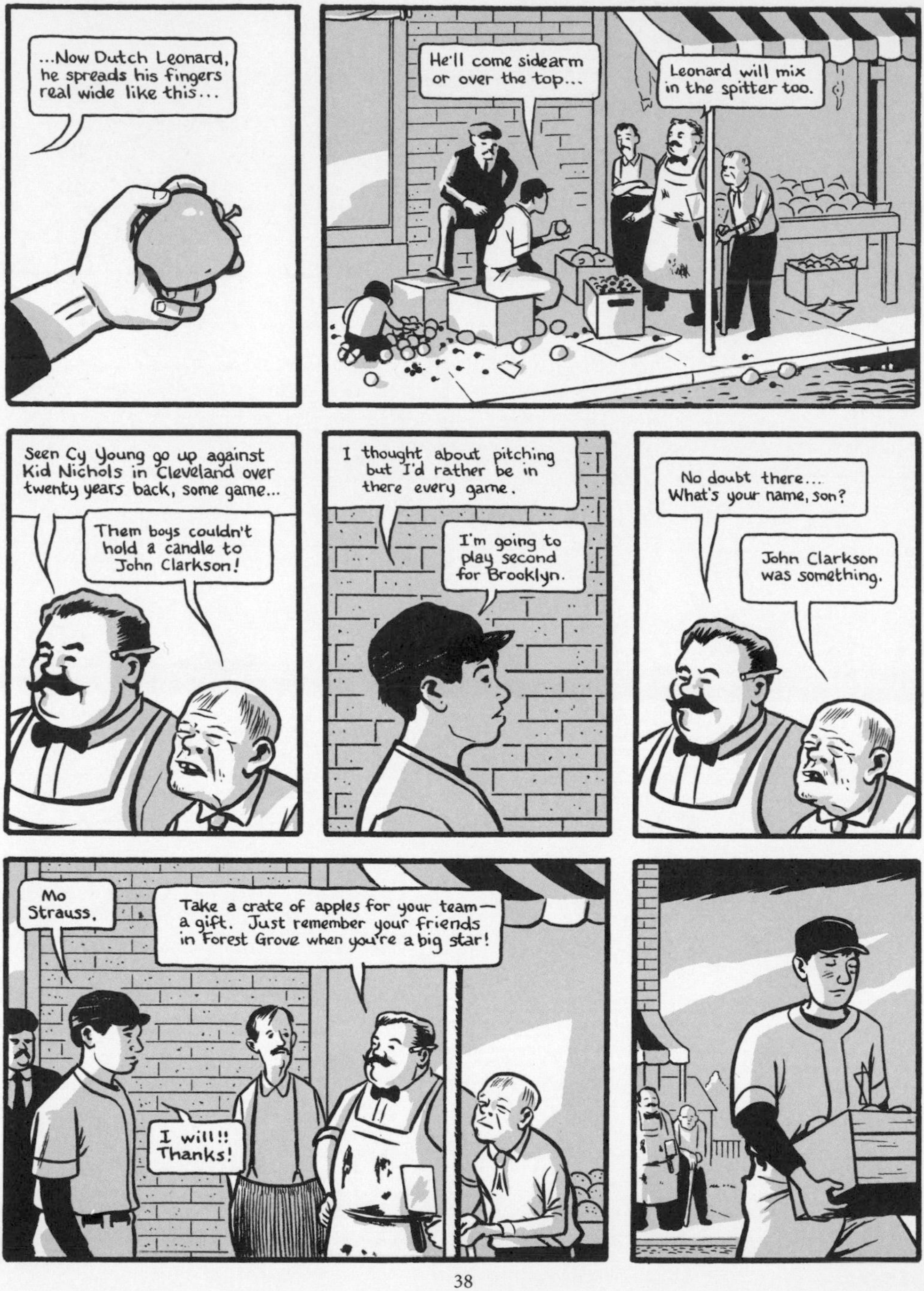
...Now Dutch Leonard, he spreads his fingers real wide like this...
He'll come sidearm or over the top...
Leonard will mix in the spitter too.
Seen Cy Young go up against Kid Nichols in Cleveland over twenty years back, some game...
Them boys couldn't hold a candle to John Clarkson!
I thought about pitching but I'd rather be in there every game.
I'm going to play second for Brooklyn.
No doubt there... What's your name, son?
John Clarkson was something.
Mo Strauss.
Take a crate of apples for your team—a gift. Just remember your friends in Forest Grove when you're a big star!
I will!! Thanks!

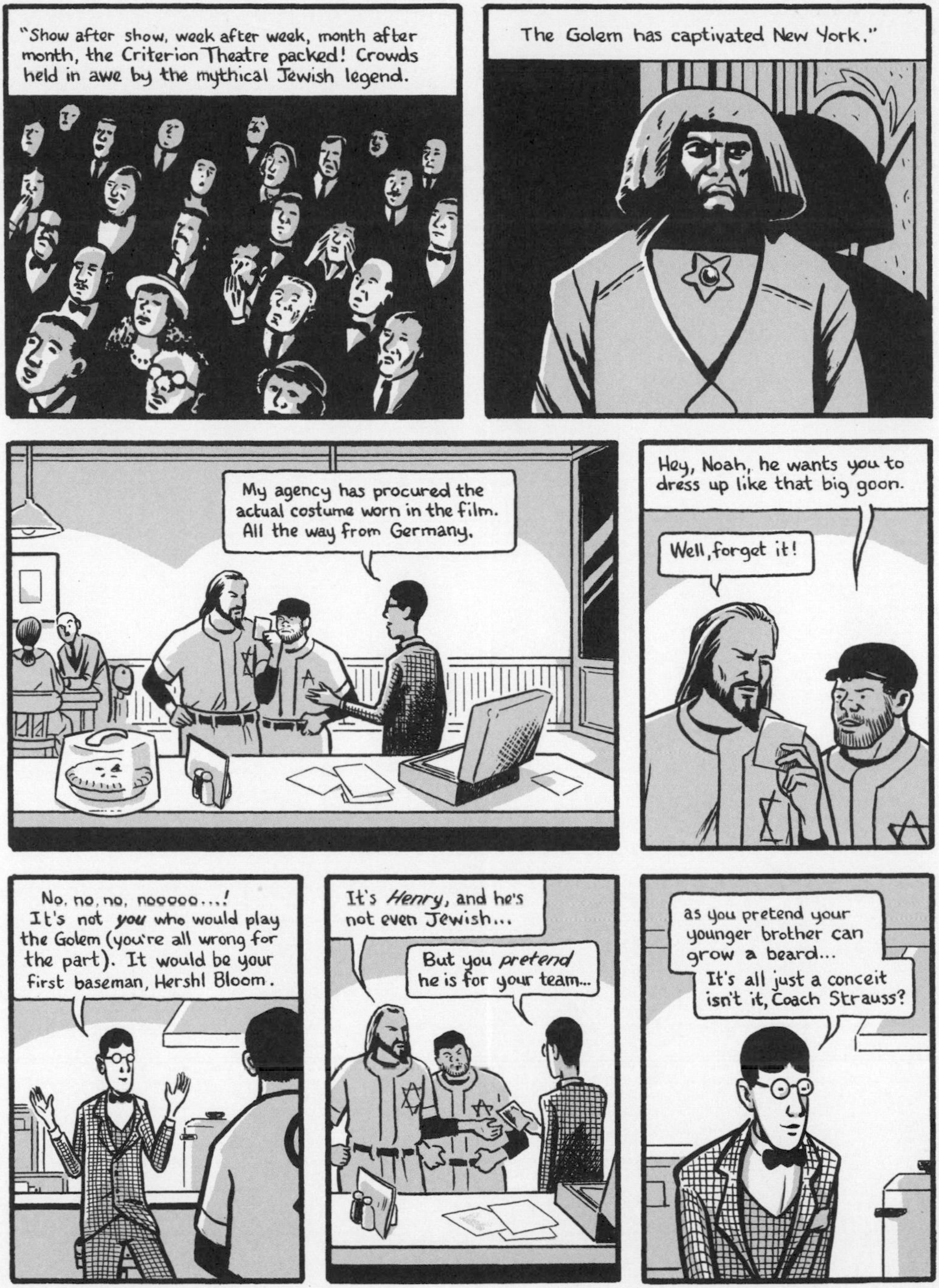
"Show after show, week after week, month after month, the Criterion Theatre packed! Crowds held in awe by the mythical Jewish legend.
The Golem has captivated New York."
My agency has procured the actual costume worn in the film. All the way from Germany.
Hey, Noah, he wants you to dress up like that big goon.
Well, forget it!
No, no, no, nooooo...! It's not *you* who would play the Golem (you're all wrong for the part). It would be your first baseman, Hershl Bloom.
It's *Henry*, and he's not even Jewish...
But you *pretend* he is for your team...
as you pretend your younger brother can grow a beard...
It's all just a conceit isn't it, Coach Strauss?

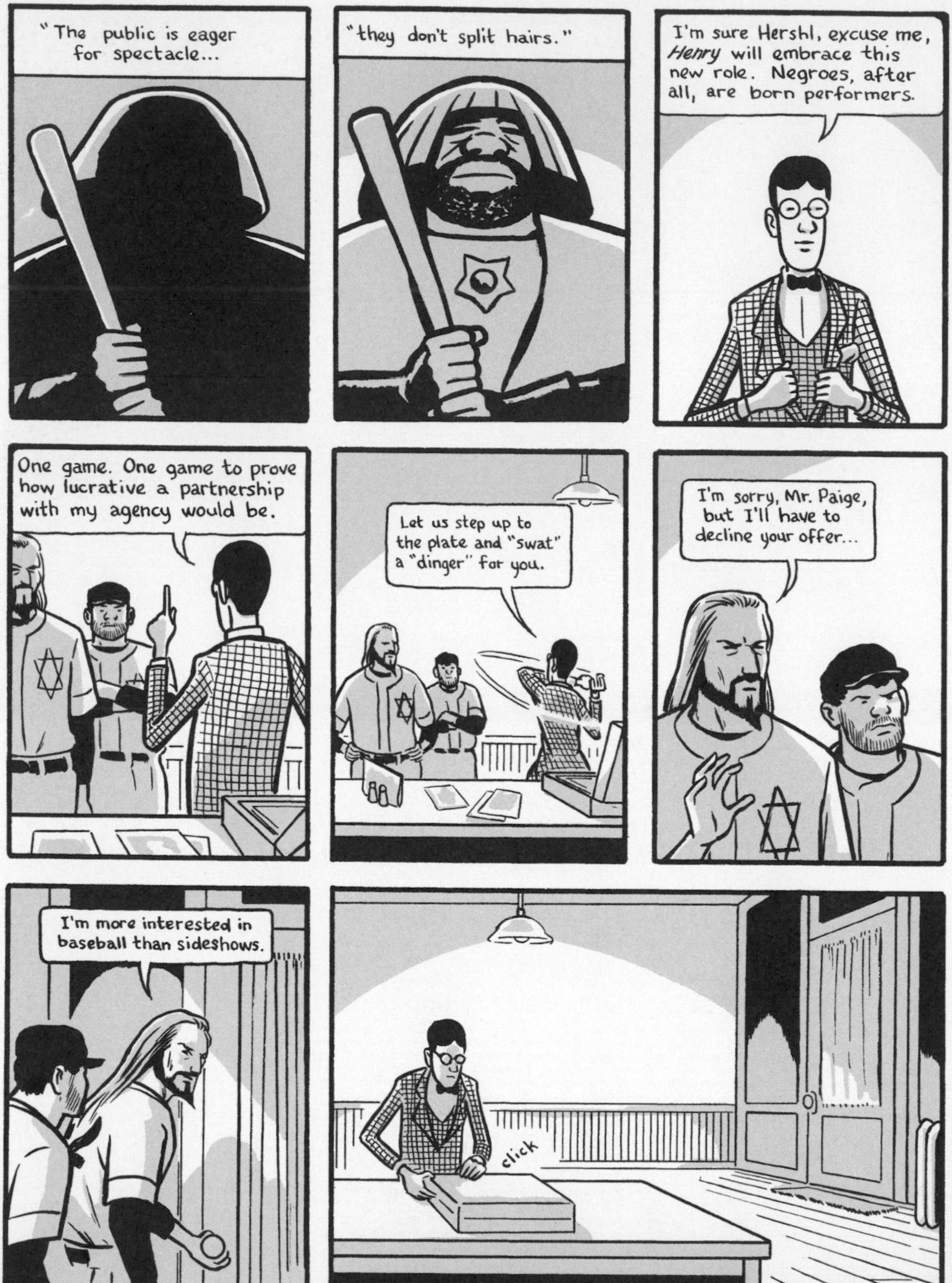
"The public is eager for spectacle...
"they don't split hairs."
I'm sure Hershl, excuse me, *Henry* will embrace this new role. Negroes, after all, are born performers.
One game. One game to prove how lucrative a partnership with my agency would be.
Let us step up to the plate and "swat" a "dinger" for you.
I'm sorry, Mr. Paige, but I'll have to decline your offer...
I'm more interested in baseball than sideshows.
click

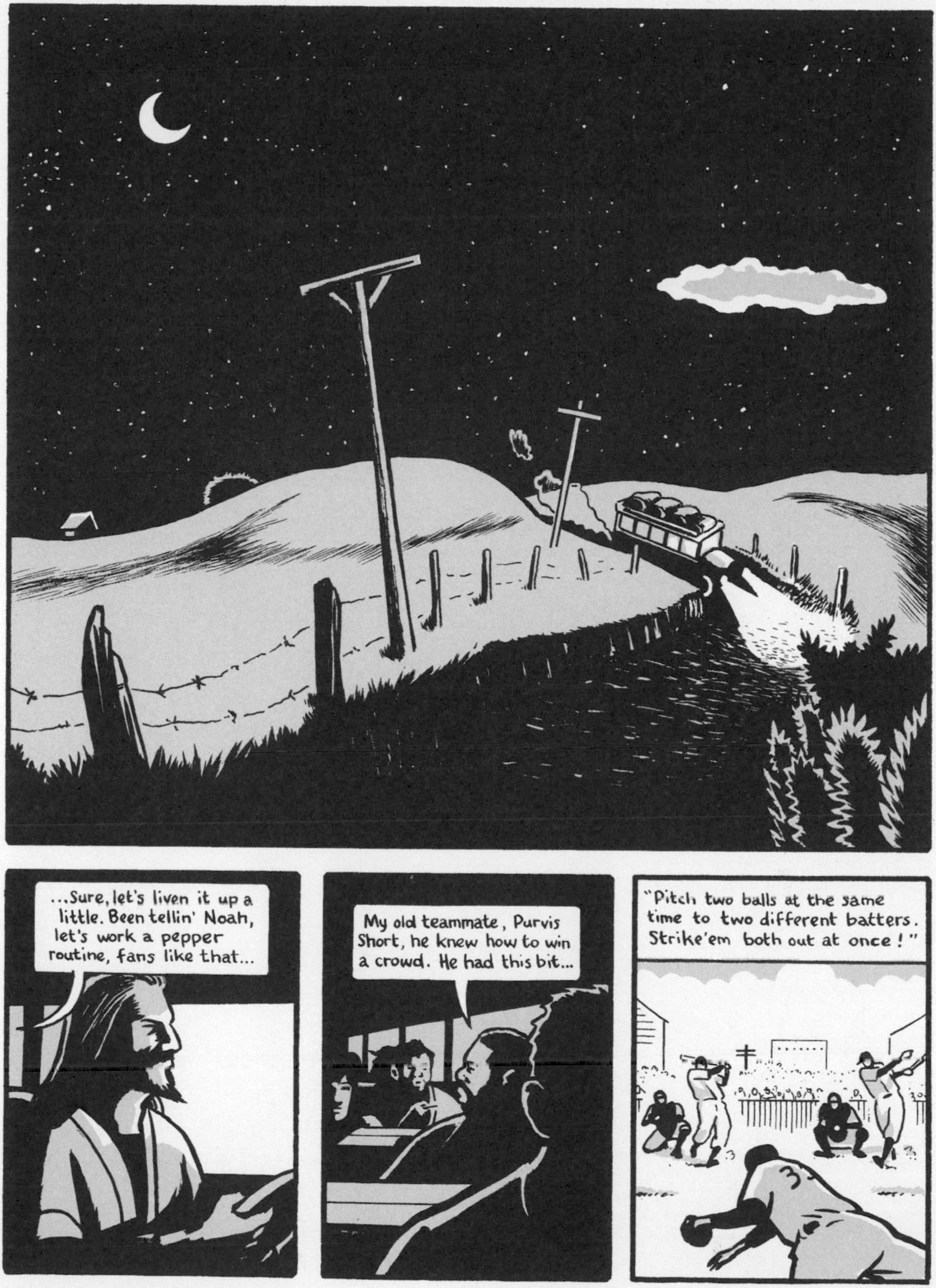
...Sure, let's liven it up a little. Been tellin' Noah, let's work a pepper routine, fans like that...
My old teammate, Purvis Short, he knew how to win a crowd. He had this bit...
"Pitch two balls at the same time to two different batters. Strike'em both out at once!"

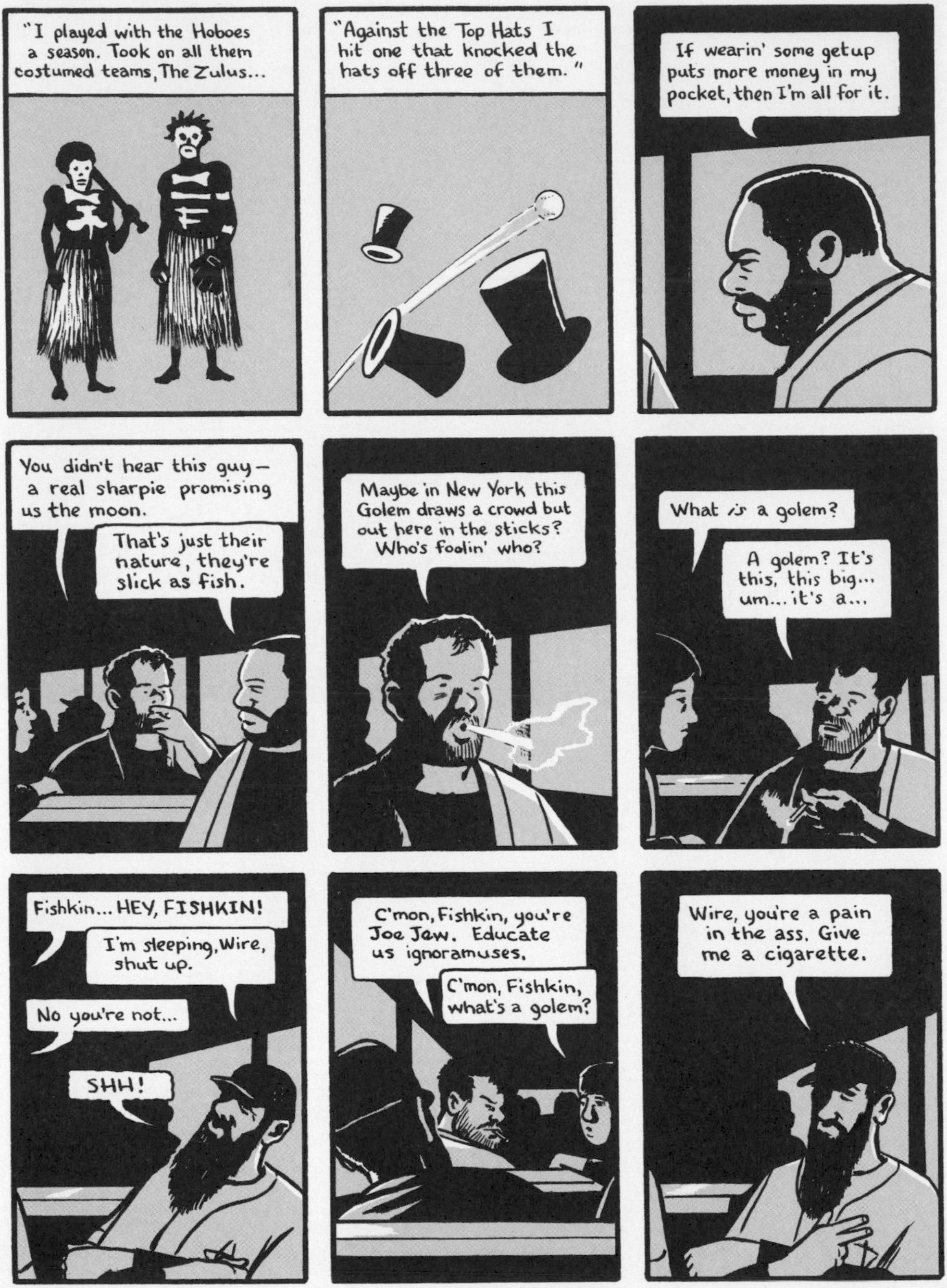
"I played with the Hoboes a season. Took on all them costumed teams, The Zulus...
"Against the Top Hats I hit one that knocked the hats off three of them."
If wearin' some getup puts more money in my pocket, then I'm all for it.
You didn't hear this guy — a real sharpie promising us the moon.
That's just their nature, they're slick as fish.
Maybe in New York this Golem draws a crowd but out here in the sticks? Who's foolin' who?
What *is* a golem?
A golem? It's this, this big... um... it's a...
Fishkin... HEY, FISHKIN!
I'm sleeping, Wire, shut up.
No you're not...
SHH!
C'mon, Fishkin, you're Joe Jew. Educate us ignoramuses.
C'mon, Fishkin, what's a golem?
Wire, you're a pain in the ass. Give me a cigarette.

"A golem is a creature that man creates to be a companion, a protector, or a servant.

"To give a golem life, esoteric rituals are performed, ancient incantations spoken. Only a kabbalist who has studied for ages possesses such knowledge.

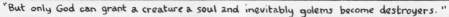

"But only God can grant a creature a soul and inevitably golems become destroyers."

What's a Kabbalist?

Most Jews only want to know what God wants from them, how to live correctly...

A kabbalist wants to discover the essence of God himself.

43

Had a humpback mascot. Won fourteen in a row when he joined the team.

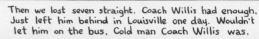

Then we lost seven straight. Coach Willis had enough. Just left him behind in Louisville one day. Wouldn't let him on the bus. Cold man Coach Willis was.

Cedar Falls, thirty miles.

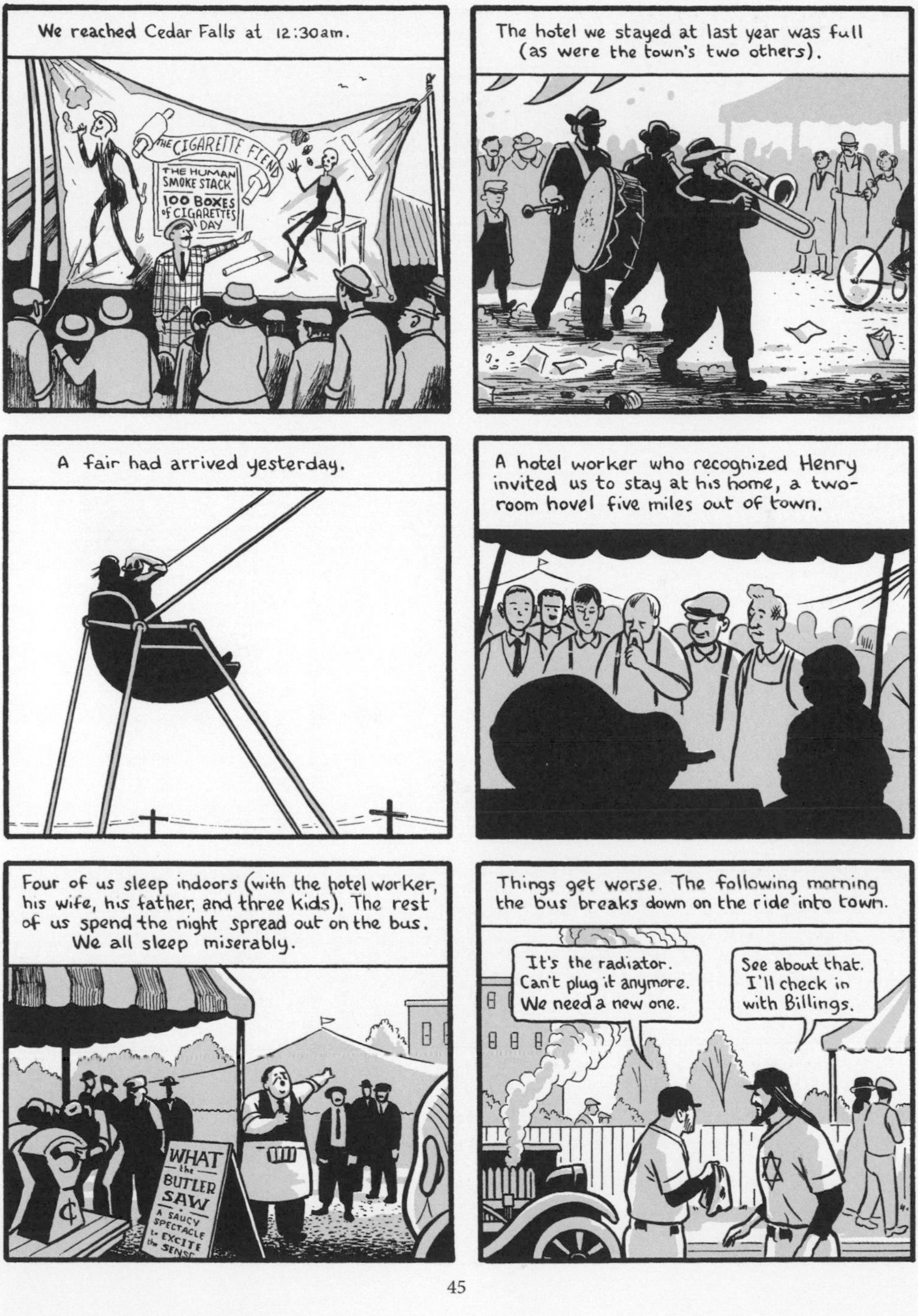
We reached Cedar Falls at 12:30am.
THE CIGARETTE FIEND
THE HUMAN SMOKE STACK
100 BOXES of CIGARETTES a DAY
The hotel we stayed at last year was full (as were the town's two others).
A fair had arrived yesterday.
A hotel worker who recognized Henry invited us to stay at his home, a two-room hovel five miles out of town.
Four of us sleep indoors (with the hotel worker, his wife, his father, and three kids). The rest of us spend the night spread out on the bus. We all sleep miserably.
WHAT the BUTLER SAW
A SAUCY SPECTACLE to EXCITE
Things get worse. The following morning the bus breaks down on the ride into town.
It's the radiator. Can't plug it anymore. We need a new one.
See about that. I'll check in with Billings.

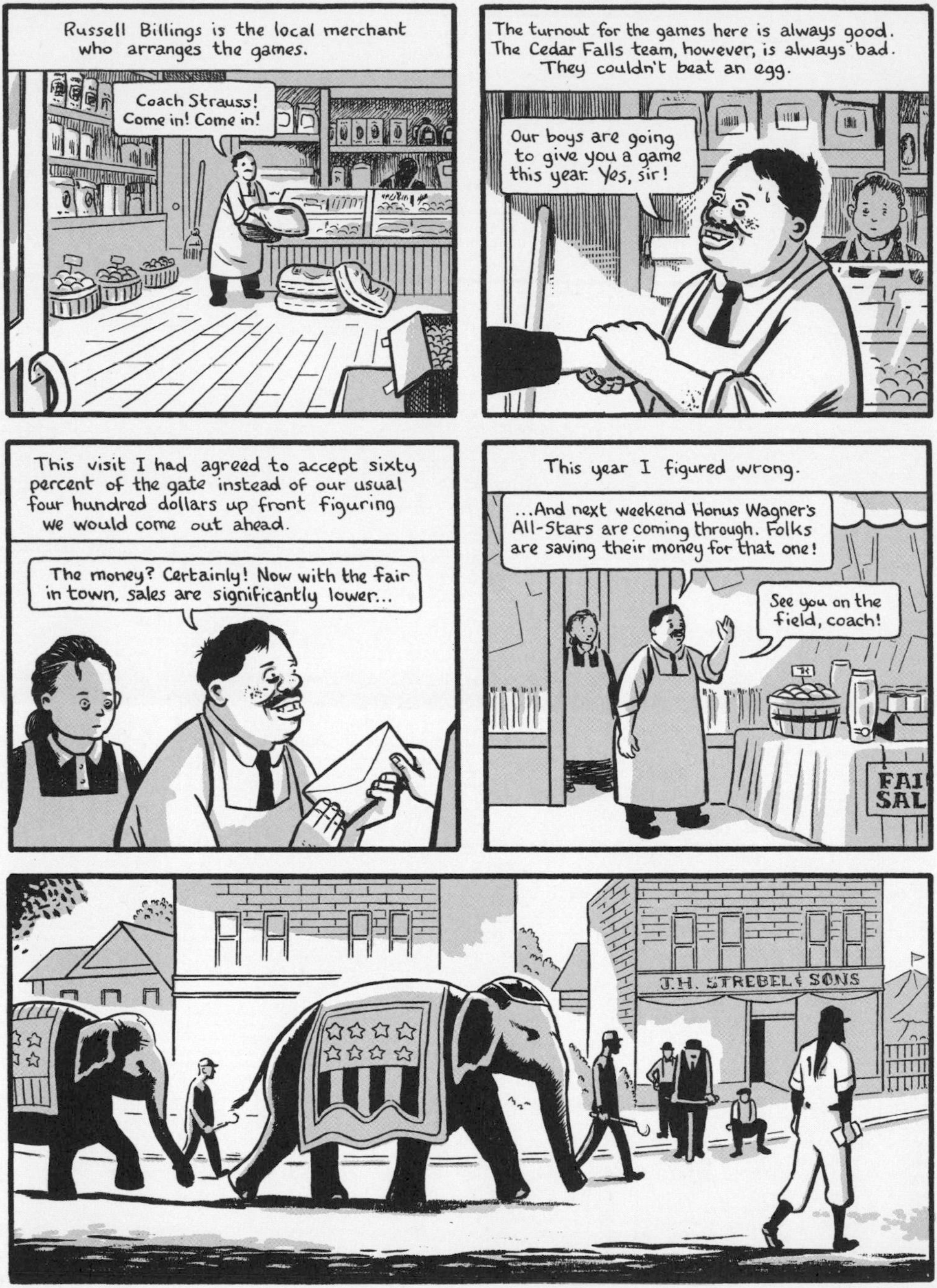
Russell Billings is the local merchant who arranges the games.
Coach Strauss! Come in! Come in!
The turnout for the games here is always good. The Cedar Falls team, however, is always bad. They couldn't beat an egg.
Our boys are going to give you a game this year. Yes, sir!
This visit I had agreed to accept sixty percent of the gate instead of our usual four hundred dollars up front figuring we would come out ahead.
The money? Certainly! Now with the fair in town, sales are significantly lower...
This year I figured wrong.
...And next weekend Honus Wagner's All-Stars are coming through. Folks are saving their money for that one!
See you on the field, coach!
J.H. STREBEL & SONS

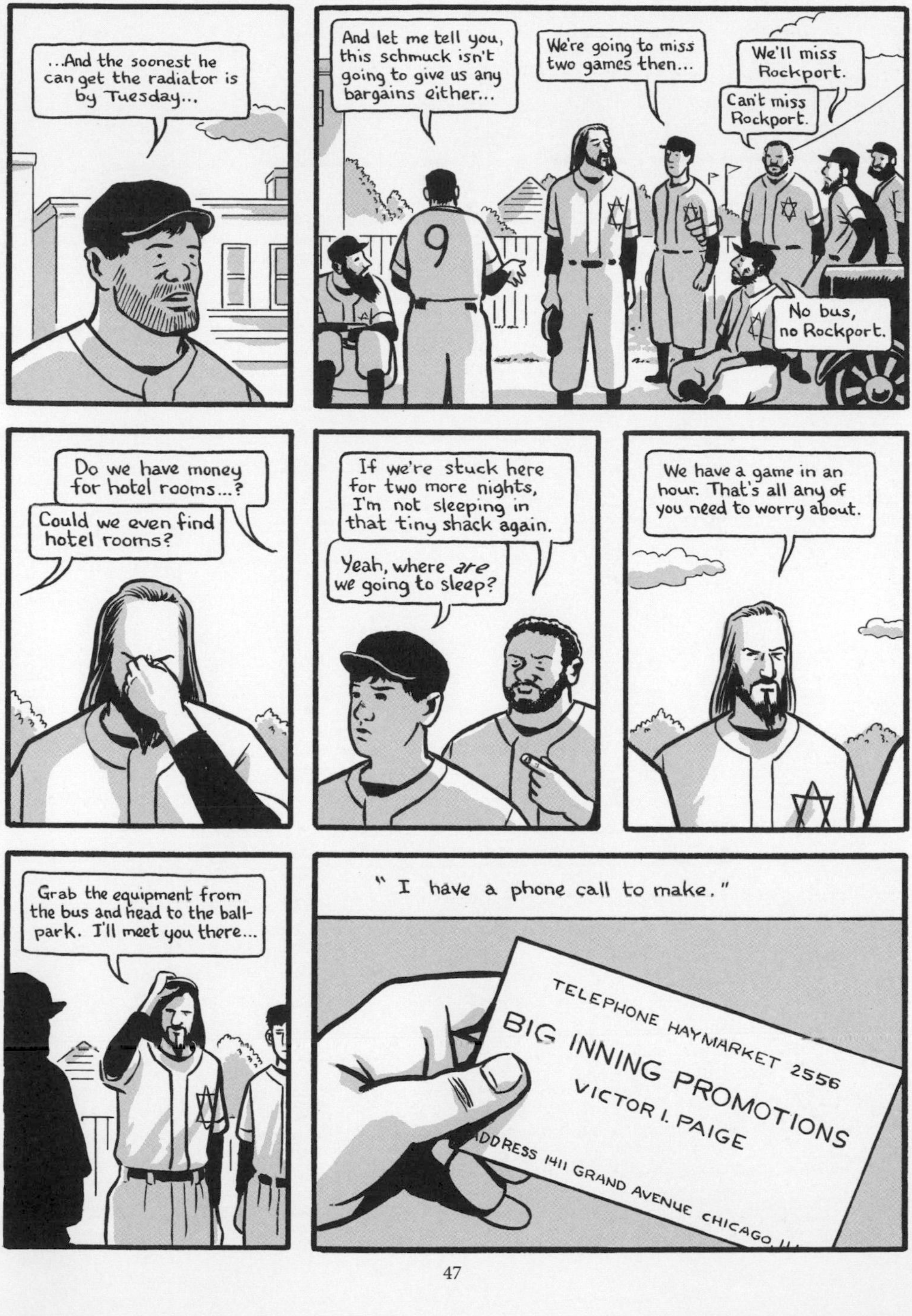
...And the soonest he can get the radiator is by Tuesday...
And let me tell you, this schmuck isn't going to give us any bargains either...
We're going to miss two games then...
We'll miss Rockport.
Can't miss Rockport.
No bus, no Rockport.
Do we have money for hotel rooms...?
Could we even find hotel rooms?
If we're stuck here for two more nights, I'm not sleeping in that tiny shack again.
Yeah, where *are* we going to sleep?
We have a game in an hour. That's all any of you need to worry about.
Grab the equipment from the bus and head to the ball-park. I'll meet you there...
" I have a phone call to make."
TELEPHONE HAYMARKET 2556
BIG INNING PROMOTIONS
VICTOR I. PAIGE
ADDRESS 1411 GRAND AVENUE CHICAGO, ILL.

BIG INNING PRODUCTIONS PRESENTS

GOLEM

THE JEWISH MEDIEVAL MONSTER! SEE HIM WITH YOUR OWN EYES!

ALONGSIDE THE STARS OF DAVID

— In Mortal Combat With —

PUTNAM ALL-AMERICANS

BASEBALL

3:00 P.M.   Saturday August 31   Admission $1.00

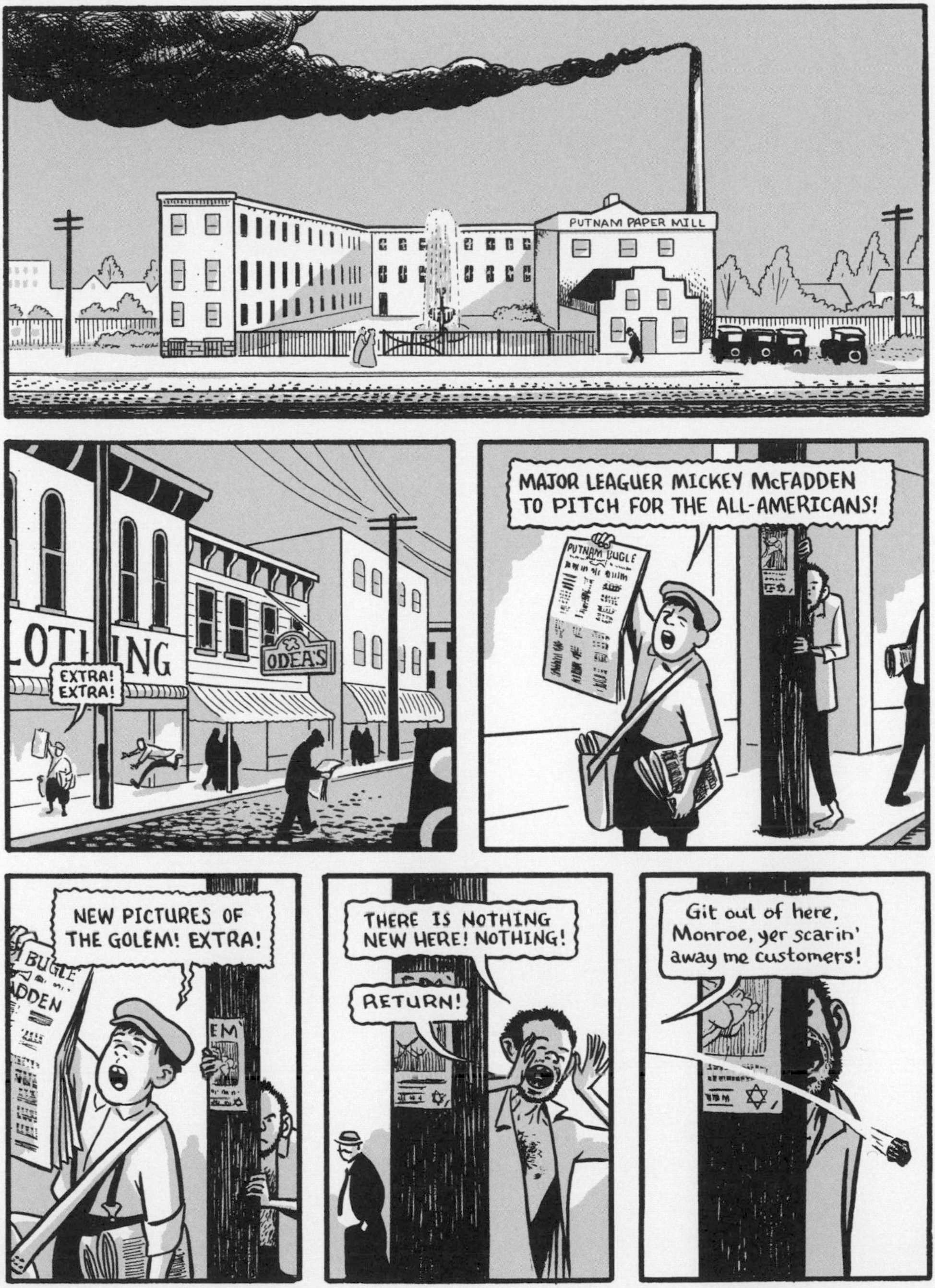
PUTNAM PAPER MILL
LOTHING
ODEA'S
EXTRA! EXTRA!
MAJOR LEAGUER MICKEY McFADDEN TO PITCH FOR THE ALL-AMERICANS!
PUTNAM BUGLE
NEW PICTURES OF THE GOLEM! EXTRA!
THERE IS NOTHING NEW HERE! NOTHING!
RETURN!
Git out of here, Monroe, yer scarin' away me customers!

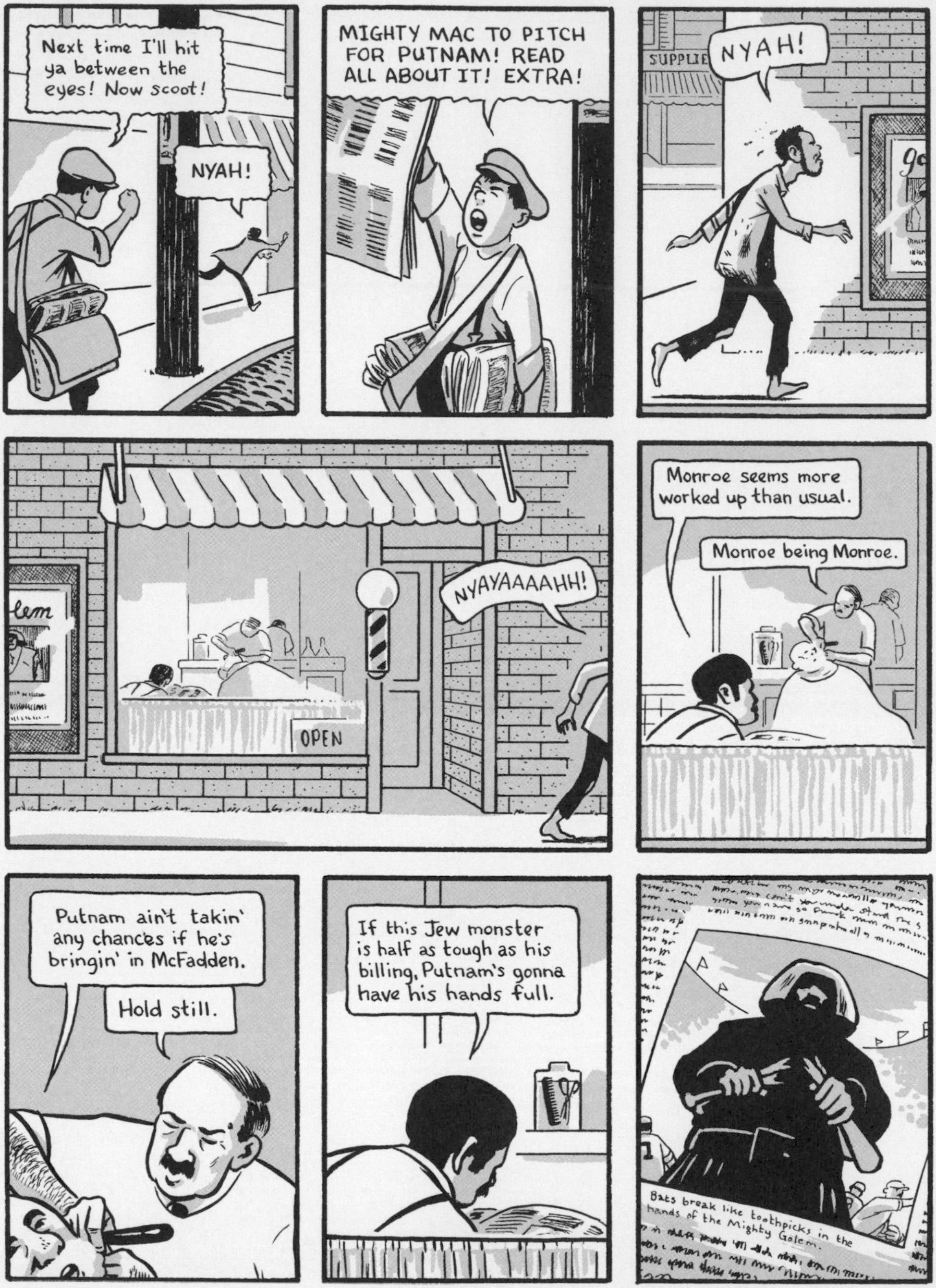

Next time I'll hit ya between the eyes! Now scoot!
NYAH!
MIGHTY MAC TO PITCH FOR PUTNAM! READ ALL ABOUT IT! EXTRA!
SUPPLIE
NYAH!
OPEN
NYAYAAAAHH!
Monroe seems more worked up than usual.
Monroe being Monroe.
Putnam ain't takin' any chances if he's bringin' in McFadden.
Hold still.
If this Jew monster is half as tough as his billing, Putnam's gonna have his hands full.
Bats break like toothpicks in the hands of the Mighty Golem.

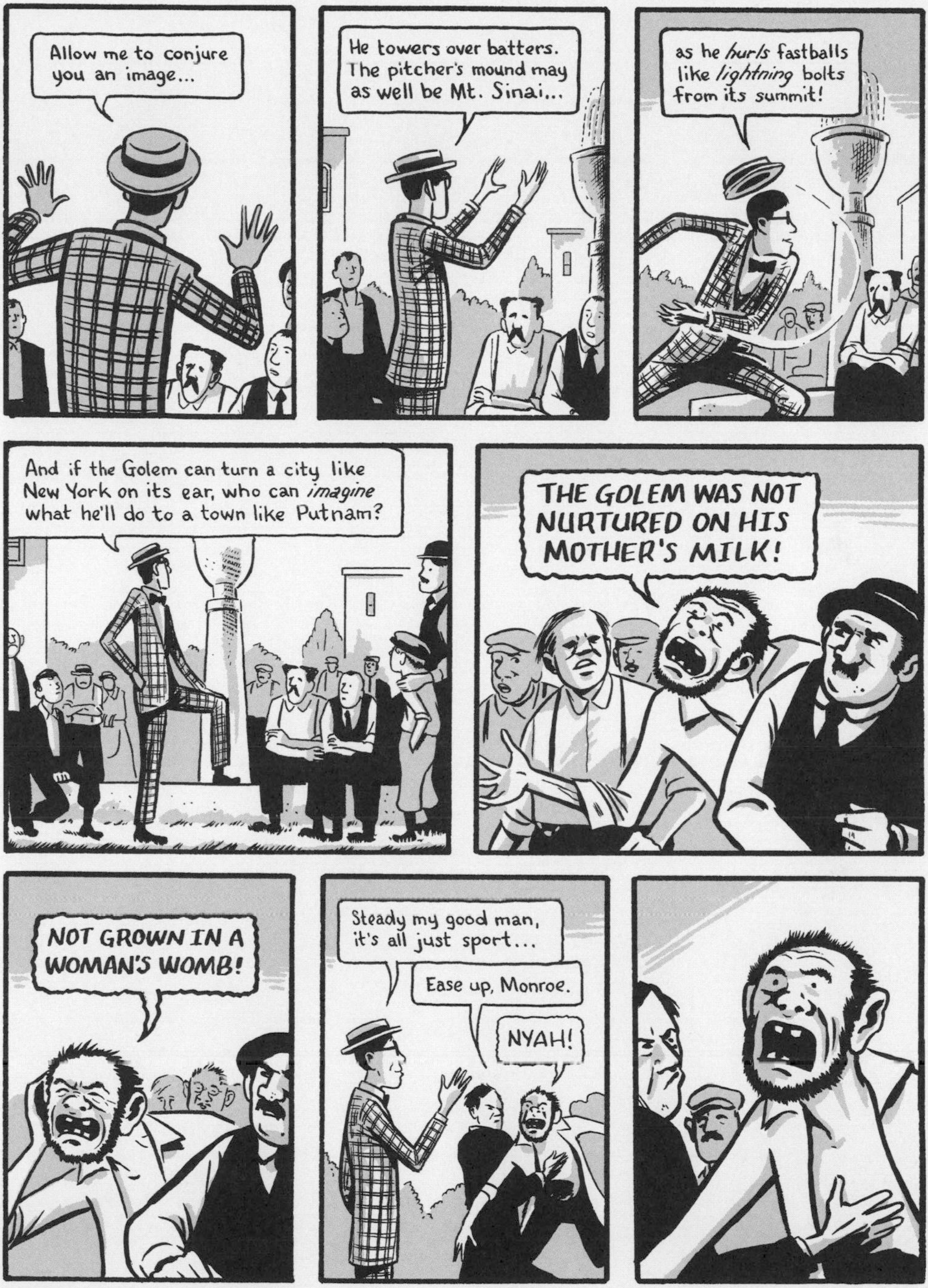
Allow me to conjure you an image...
He towers over batters. The pitcher's mound may as well be Mt. Sinai...
as he *hurls* fastballs like *lightning* bolts from its summit!
And if the Golem can turn a city like New York on its ear, who can *imagine* what he'll do to a town like Putnam?
THE GOLEM WAS NOT NURTURED ON HIS MOTHER'S MILK!
NOT GROWN IN A WOMAN'S WOMB!
Steady my good man, it's all just sport...
Ease up, Monroe.
NYAH!

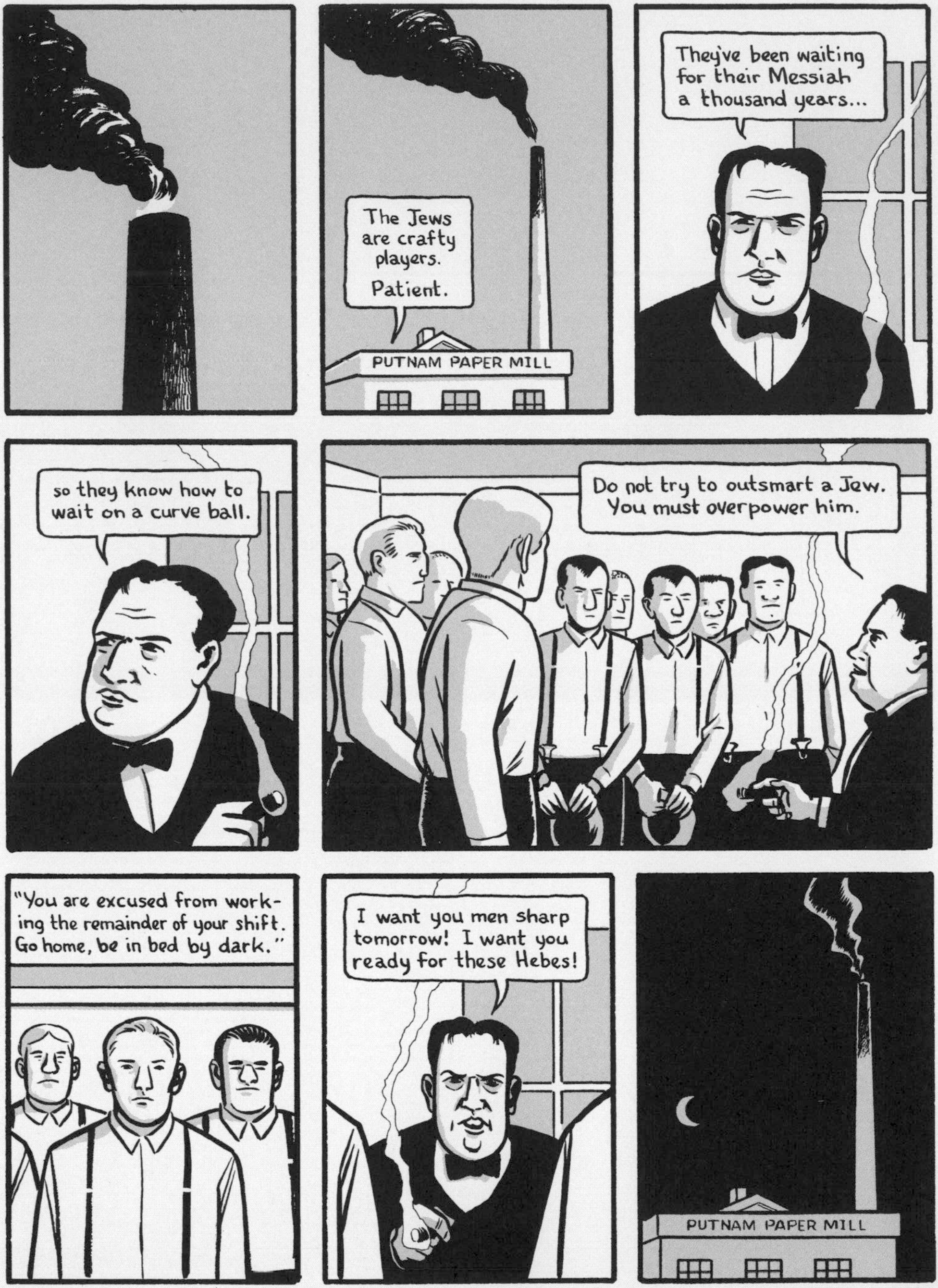

PUTNAM PAPER MILL
The Jews are crafty players.
Patient.
They've been waiting for their Messiah a thousand years...
so they know how to wait on a curve ball.
Do not try to outsmart a Jew. You must overpower him.
"You are excused from working the remainder of your shift. Go home, be in bed by dark."
I want you men sharp tomorrow! I want you ready for these Hebes!
PUTNAM PAPER MILL

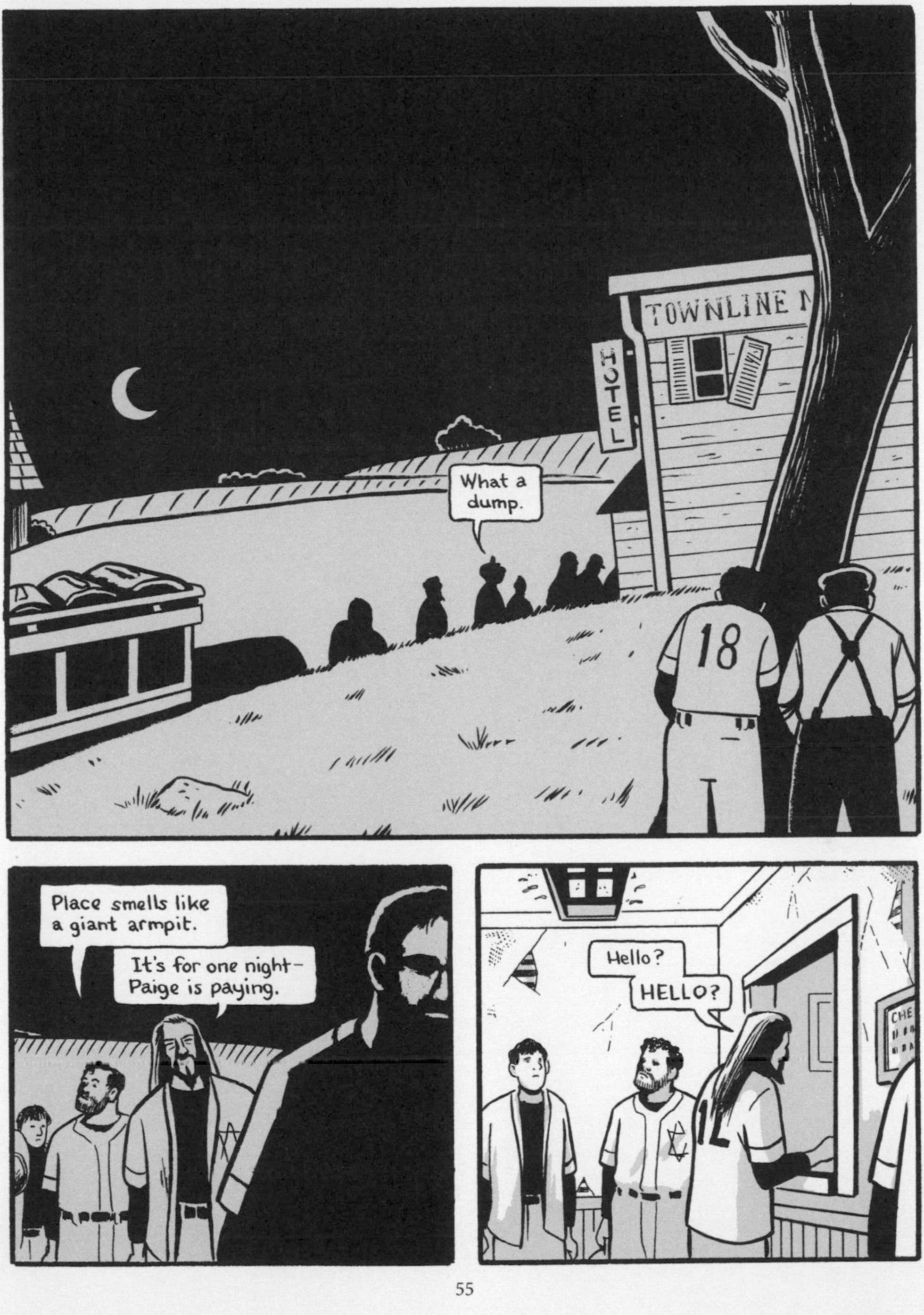
TOWNLINE M
HOTEL
What a dump.
18
Place smells like a giant armpit.
It's for one night-Paige is paying.
Hello?
HELLO?
CHE

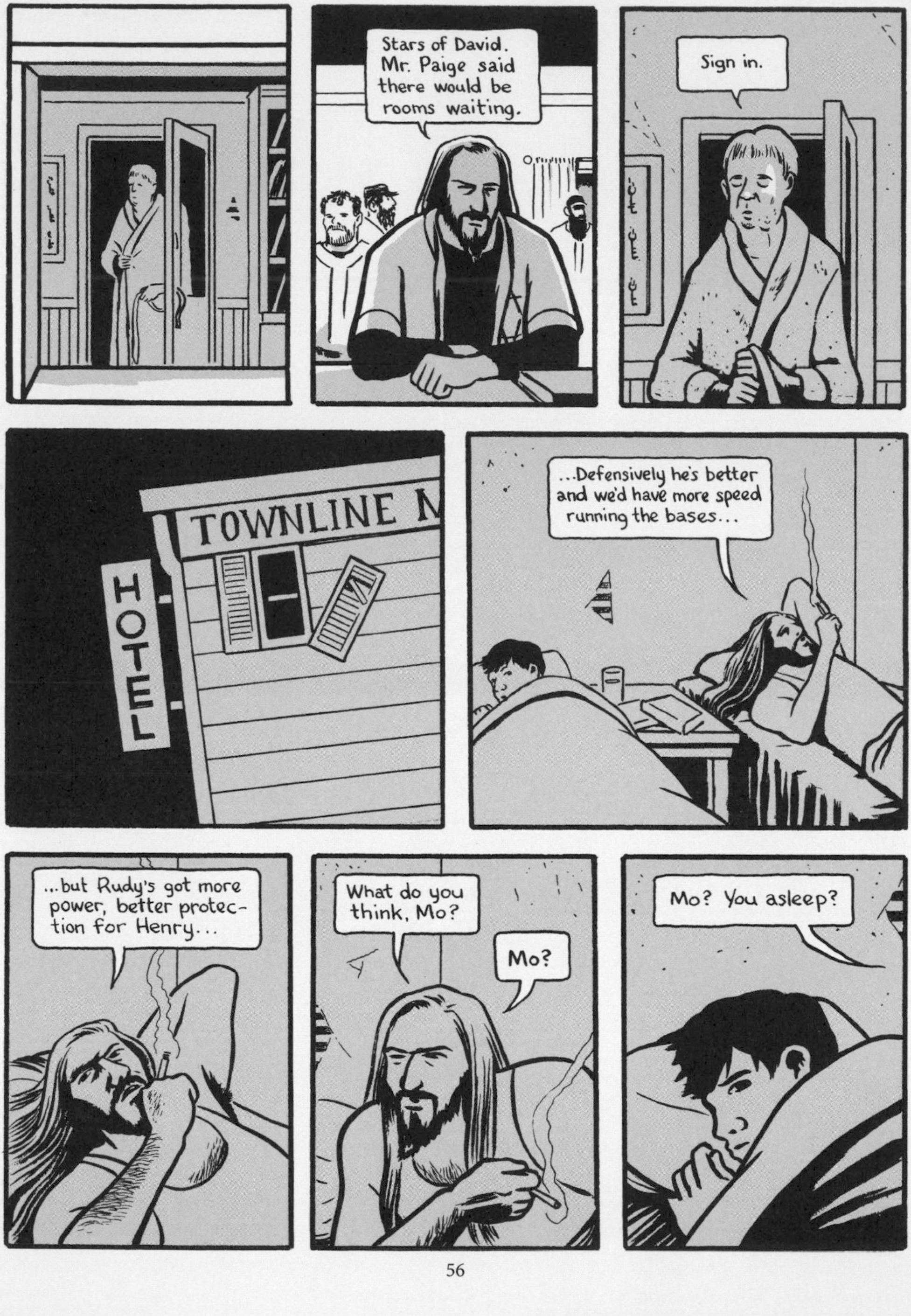

Stars of David. Mr. Paige said there would be rooms waiting.
Sign in.
TOWNLINE M
HOTEL
...Defensively he's better and we'd have more speed running the bases...
...but Rudy's got more power, better protec-tion for Henry...
What do you think, Mo?
Mo?
Mo? You asleep?

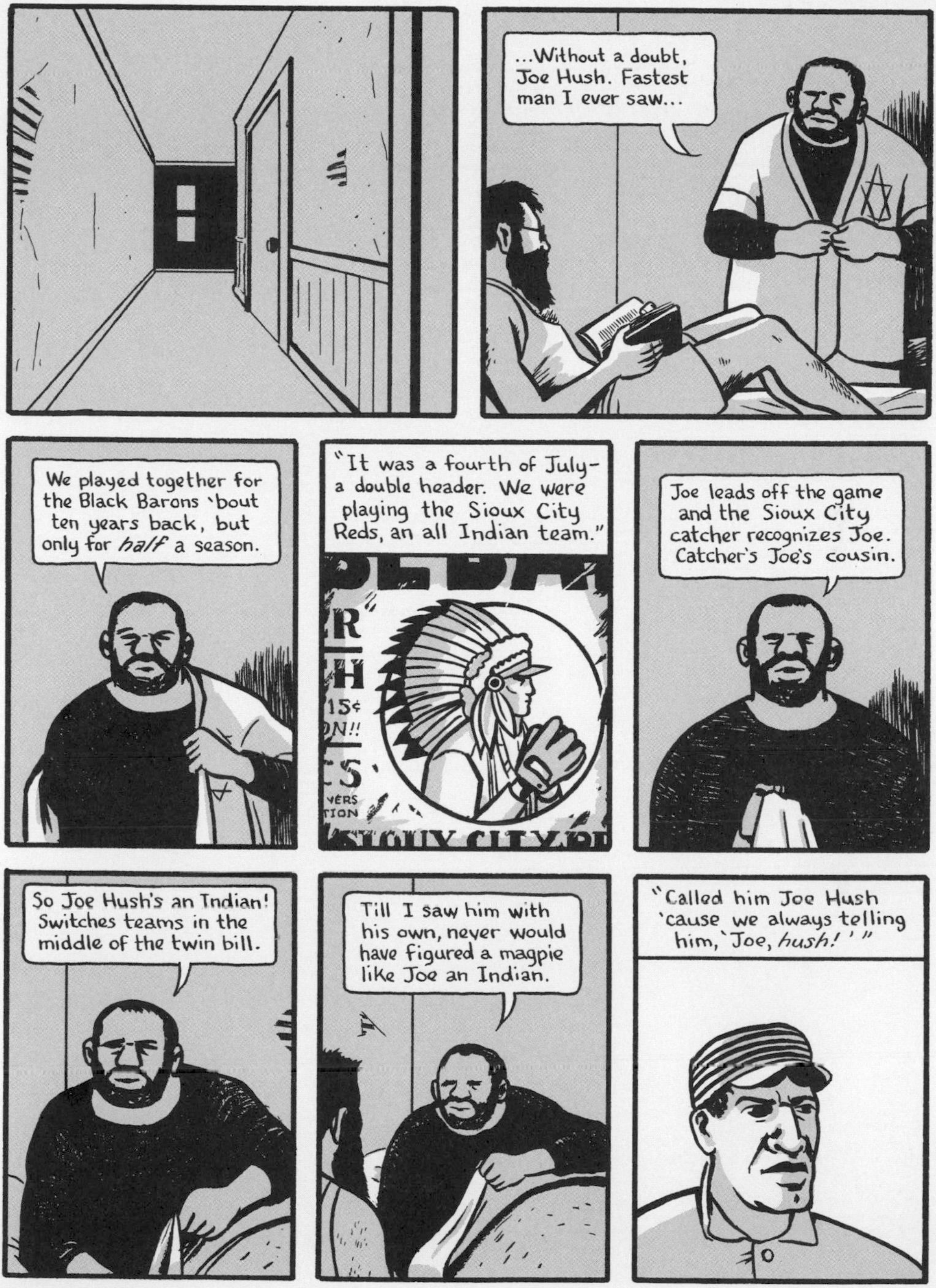
...Without a doubt, Joe Hush. Fastest man I ever saw...
We played together for the Black Barons 'bout ten years back, but only for *half* a season.
"It was a fourth of July-a double header. We were playing the Sioux City Reds, an all Indian team."
Joe leads off the game and the Sioux City catcher recognizes Joe. Catcher's Joe's cousin.
So Joe Hush's an Indian! Switches teams in the middle of the twin bill.
Till I saw him with his own, never would have figured a magpie like Joe an Indian.
"Called him Joe Hush 'cause we always telling him, 'Joe, *hush!*'"

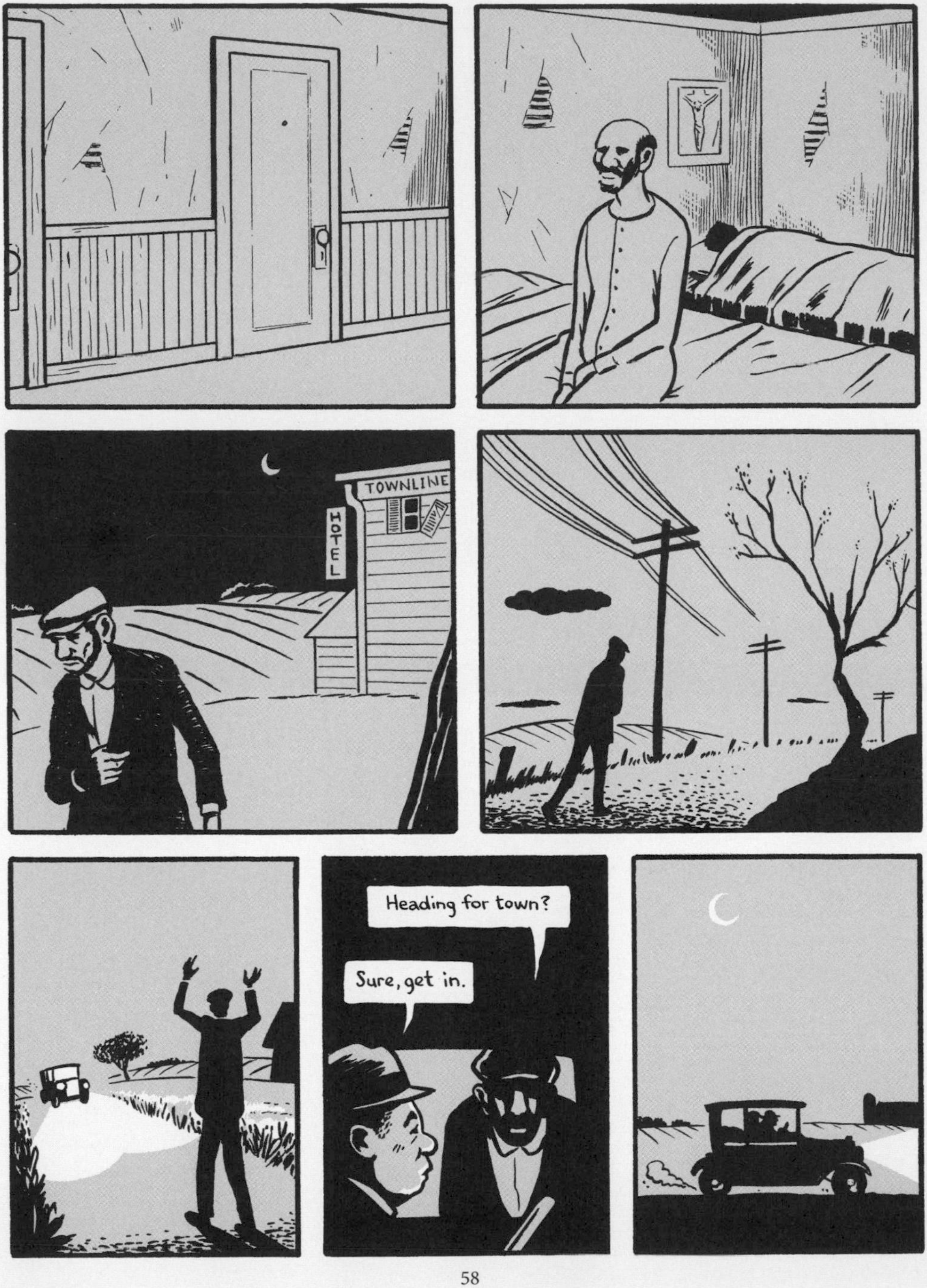
TOWNLINE
HOTEL
Heading for town?
Sure, get in.

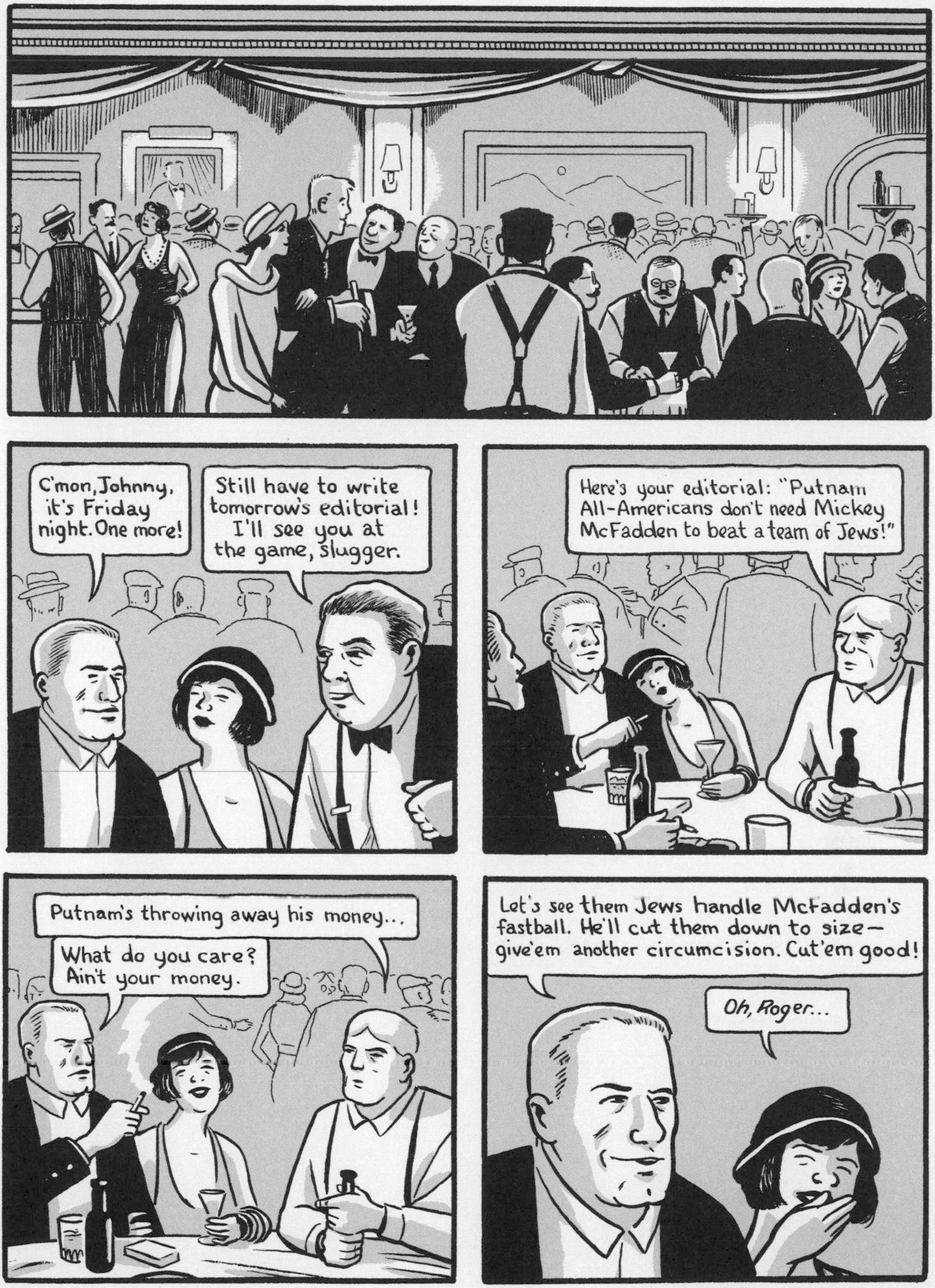
C'mon, Johnny, it's Friday night. One more!
Still have to write tomorrow's editorial! I'll see you at the game, slugger.
Here's your editorial: "Putnam All-Americans don't need Mickey McFadden to beat a team of Jews!"
Putnam's throwing away his money...
What do you care? Ain't your money.
Let's see them Jews handle McFadden's fastball. He'll cut them down to size— give'em another circumcision. Cut'em good!
Oh, Roger...

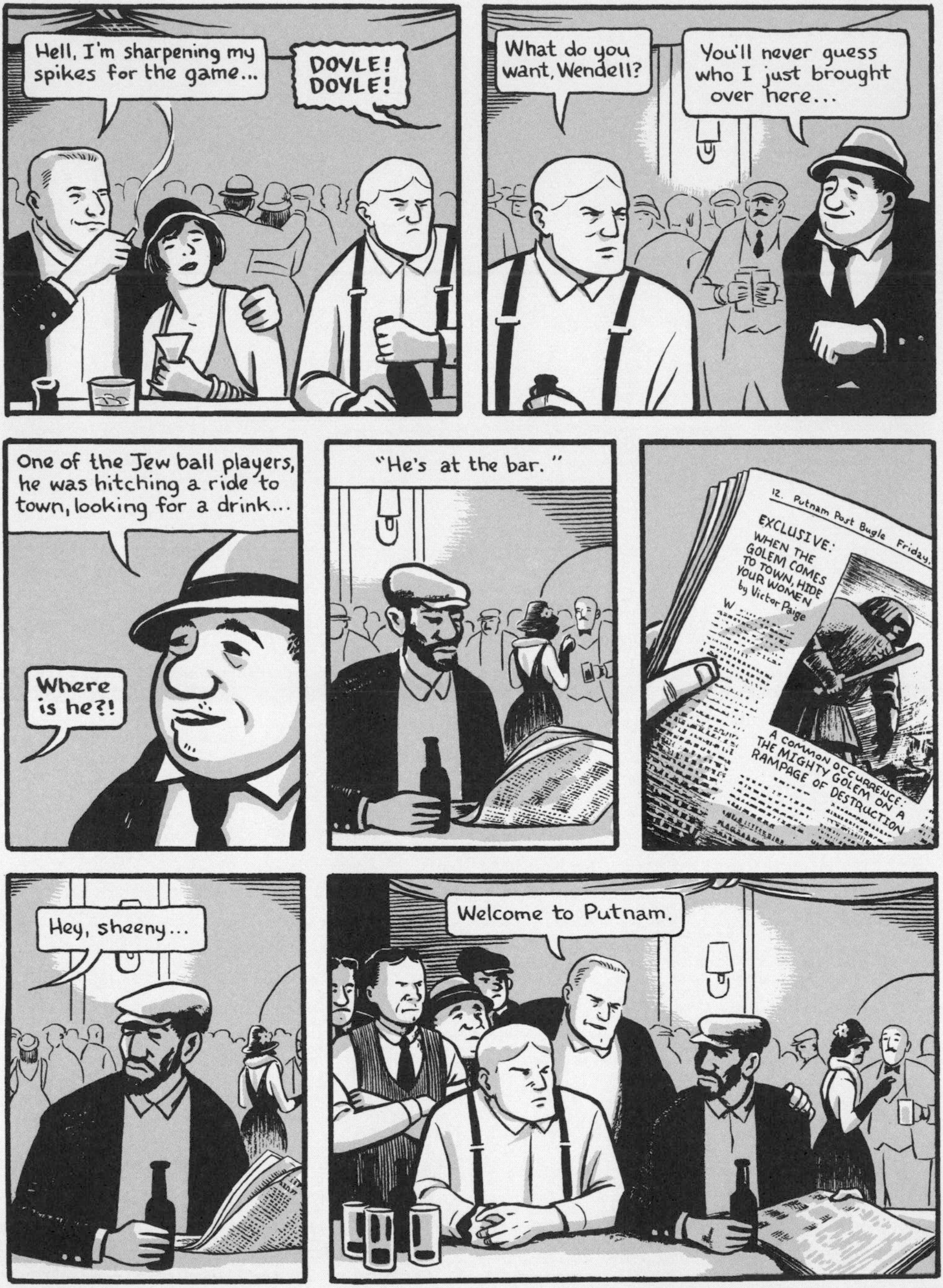

Hell, I'm sharpening my spikes for the game...
DOYLE! DOYLE!
What do you want, Wendell?
You'll never guess who I just brought over here...
One of the Jew ball players, he was hitching a ride to town, looking for a drink...
Where is he?!
"He's at the bar."
12. Putnam Post Bugle Friday.
EXCLUSIVE: WHEN THE GOLEM COMES TO TOWN, HIDE YOUR WOMEN
by Victor Paige
A COMMON OCCURRENCE: THE MIGHTY GOLEM ON A RAMPAGE OF DESTRUCTION
Hey, sheeny...
Welcome to Putnam.

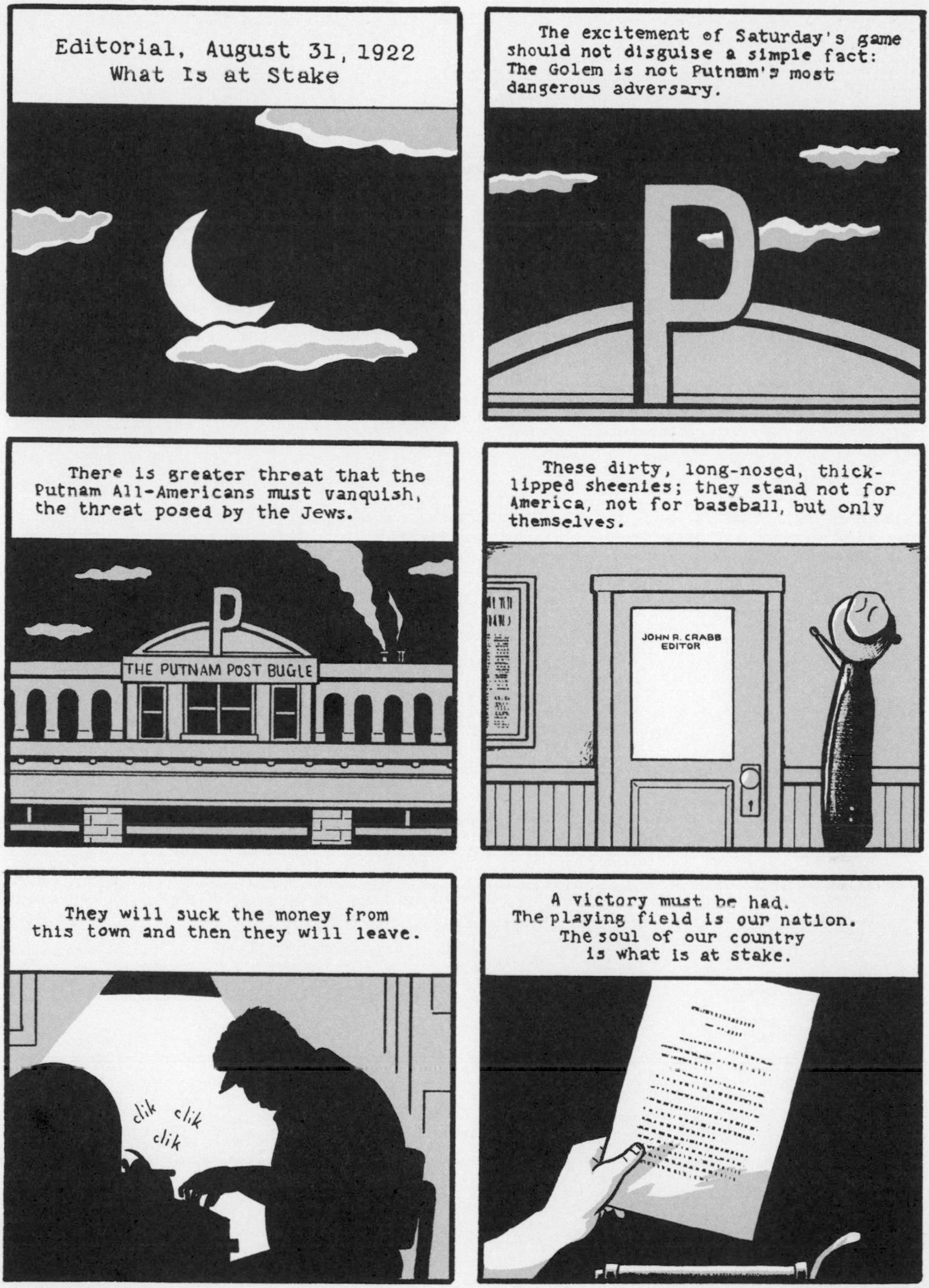
Editorial, August 31, 1922
What Is at Stake
The excitement of Saturday's game should not disguise a simple fact: The Golem is not Putnam's most dangerous adversary.
There is greater threat that the Putnam All-Americans must vanquish, the threat posed by the Jews.
THE PUTNAM POST BUGLE
These dirty, long-nosed, thick-lipped sheenies; they stand not for America, not for baseball, but only themselves.
JOHN R. CRABB
EDITOR
They will suck the money from this town and then they will leave.
clik clik
clik
A victory must be had.
The playing field is our nation.
The soul of our country
is what is at stake.

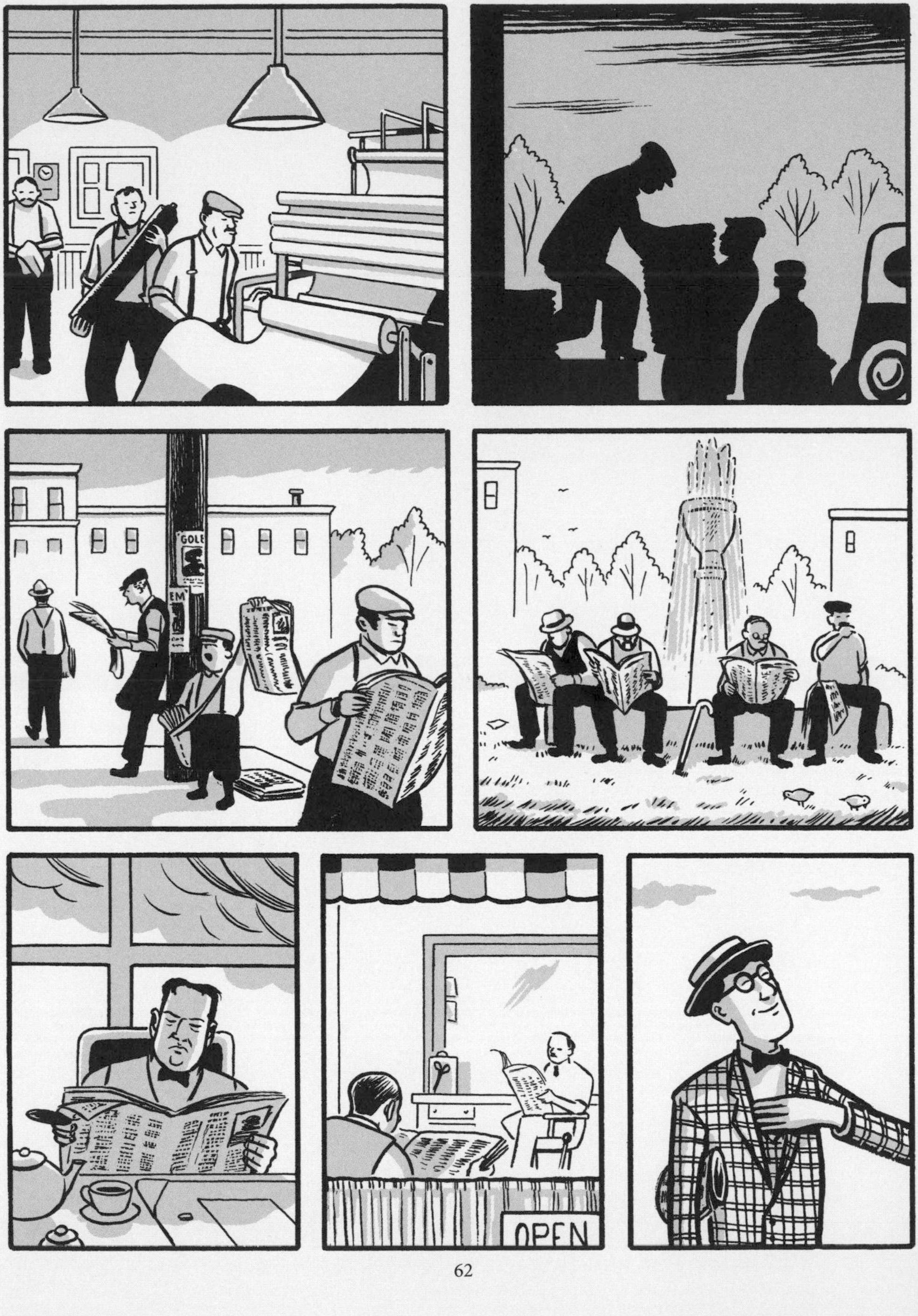
OPEN

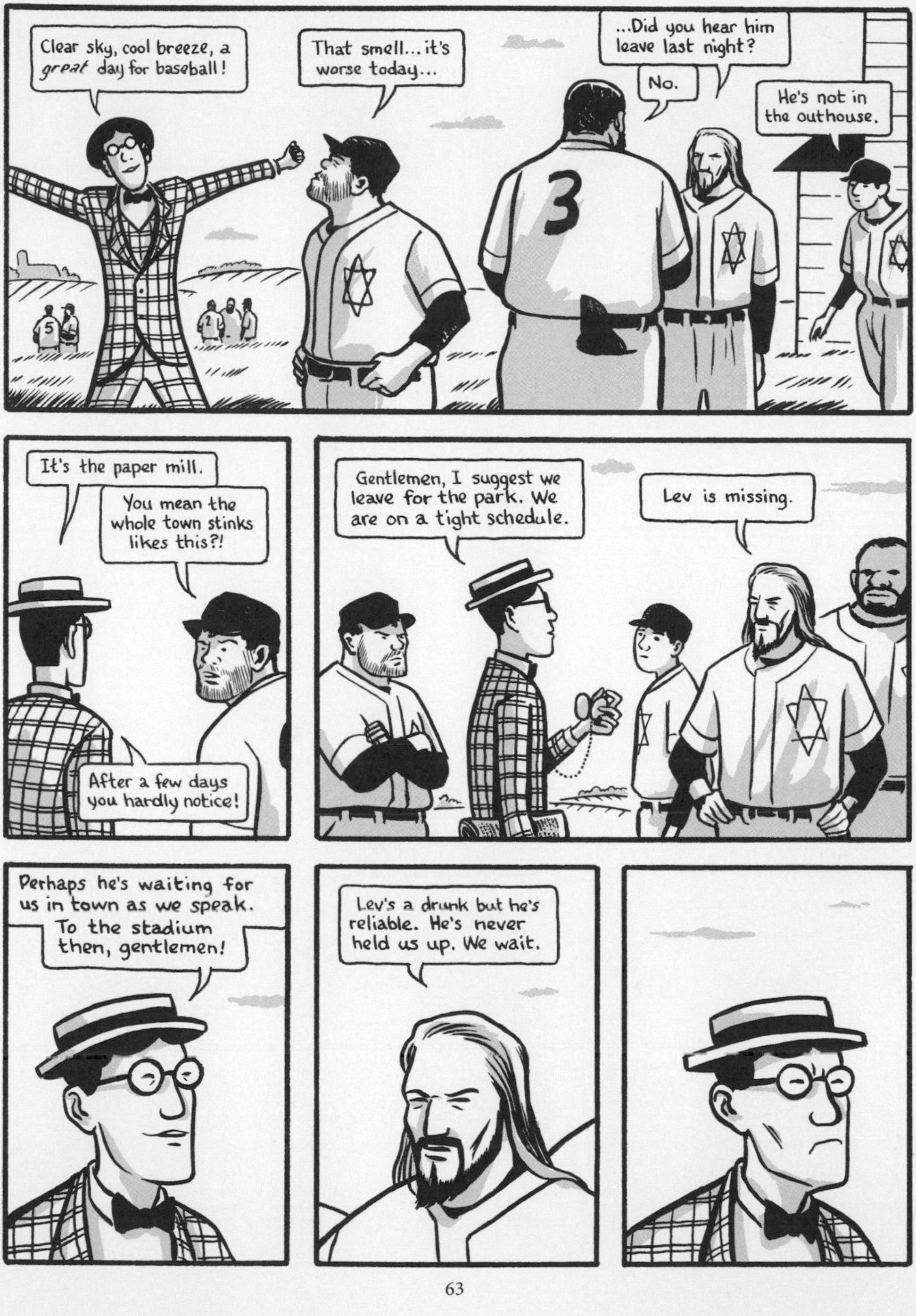
Clear sky, cool breeze, a *great* day for baseball!
That smell... it's worse today...
...Did you hear him leave last night?
No.
He's not in the outhouse.
It's the paper mill.
You mean the whole town stinks likes this?!
After a few days you hardly notice!
Gentlemen, I suggest we leave for the park. We are on a tight schedule.
Lev is missing.
Perhaps he's waiting for us in town as we speak. To the stadium then, gentlemen!
Lev's a drunk but he's reliable. He's never held us up. We wait.

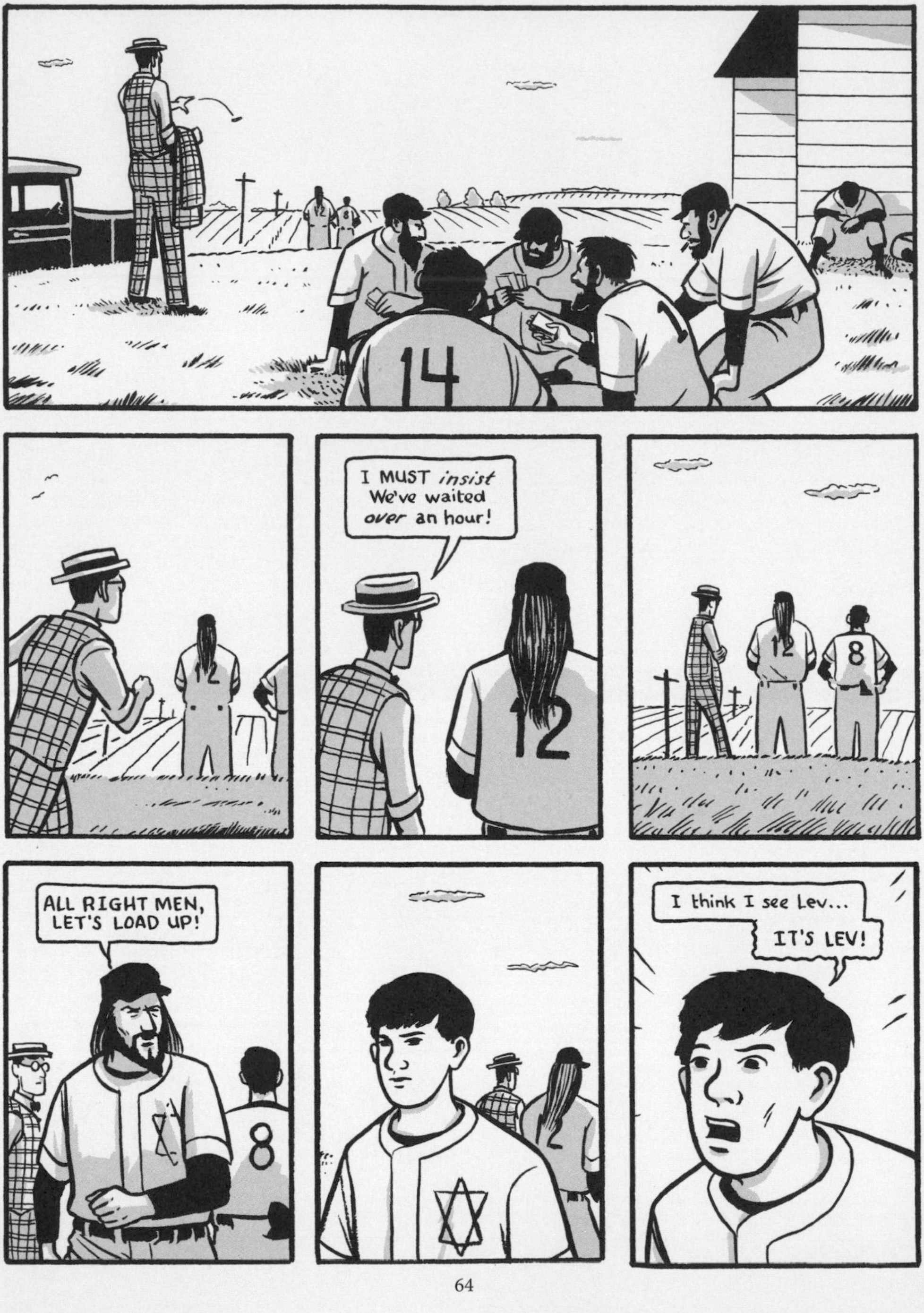
I MUST insist We've waited over an hour!
ALL RIGHT MEN, LET'S LOAD UP!
I think I see Lev...
IT'S LEV!

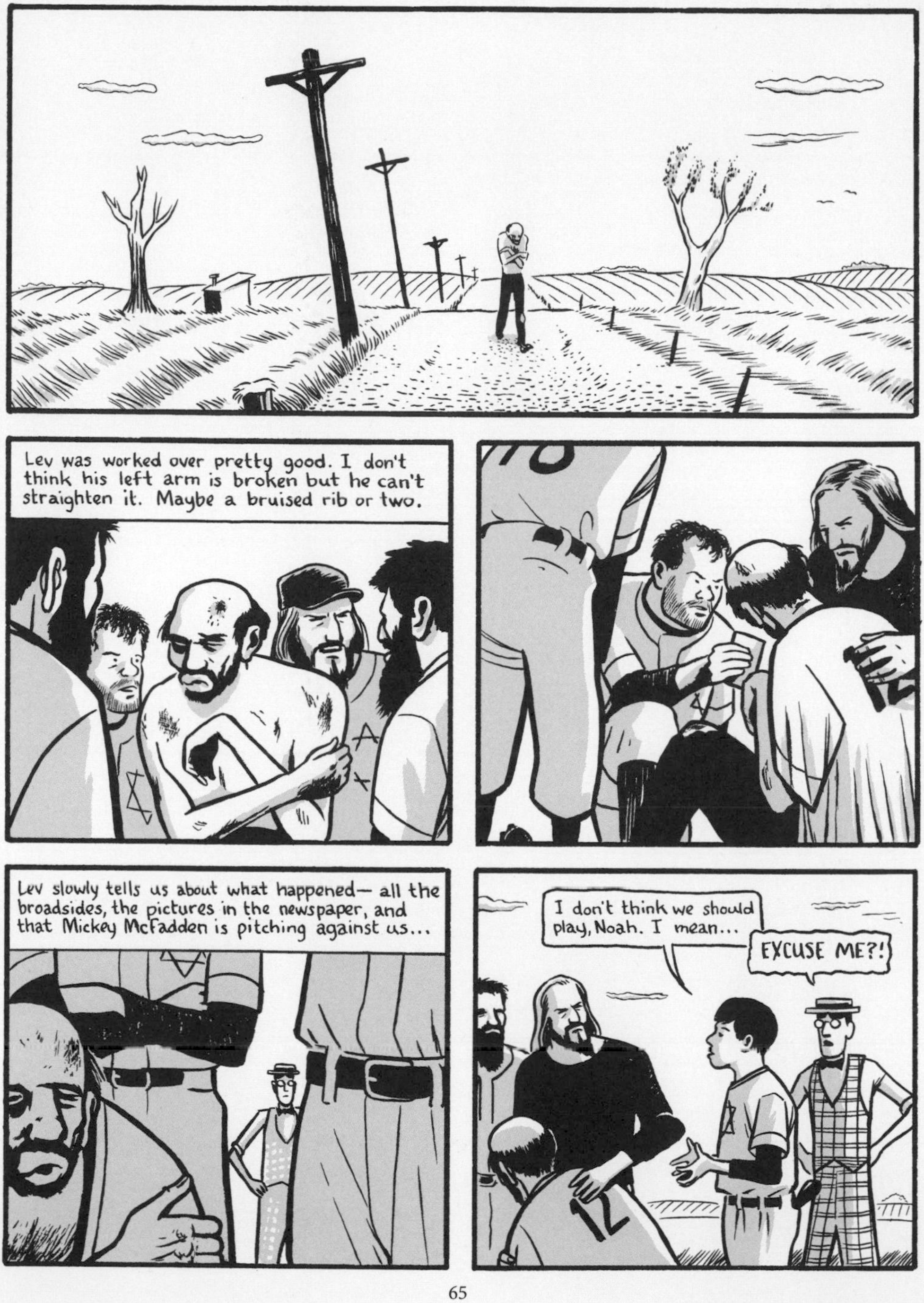
Lev was worked over pretty good. I don't think his left arm is broken but he can't straighten it. Maybe a bruised rib or two.
Lev slowly tells us about what happened— all the broadsides, the pictures in the newspaper, and that Mickey McFadden is pitching against us...
I don't think we should play, Noah. I mean...
EXCUSE ME?!

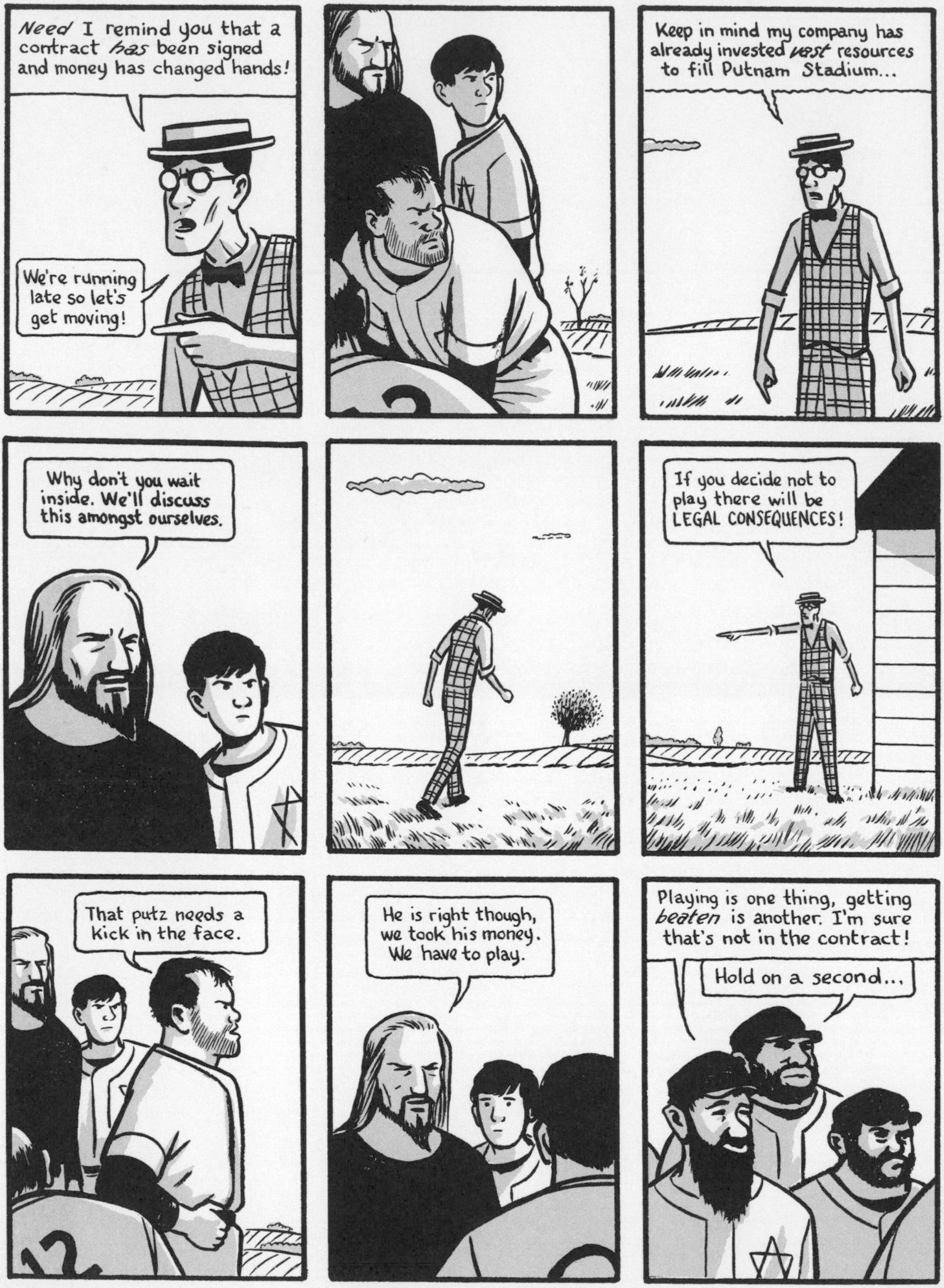
Need I remind you that a contract has been signed and money has changed hands!
We're running late so let's get moving!
Keep in mind my company has already invested vest resources to fill Putnam Stadium...
Why don't you wait inside. We'll discuss this amongst ourselves.
If you decide not to play there will be LEGAL CONSEQUENCES!
That putz needs a kick in the face.
He is right though, we took his money. We have to play.
Playing is one thing, getting beaten is another. I'm sure that's not in the contract!
Hold on a second...

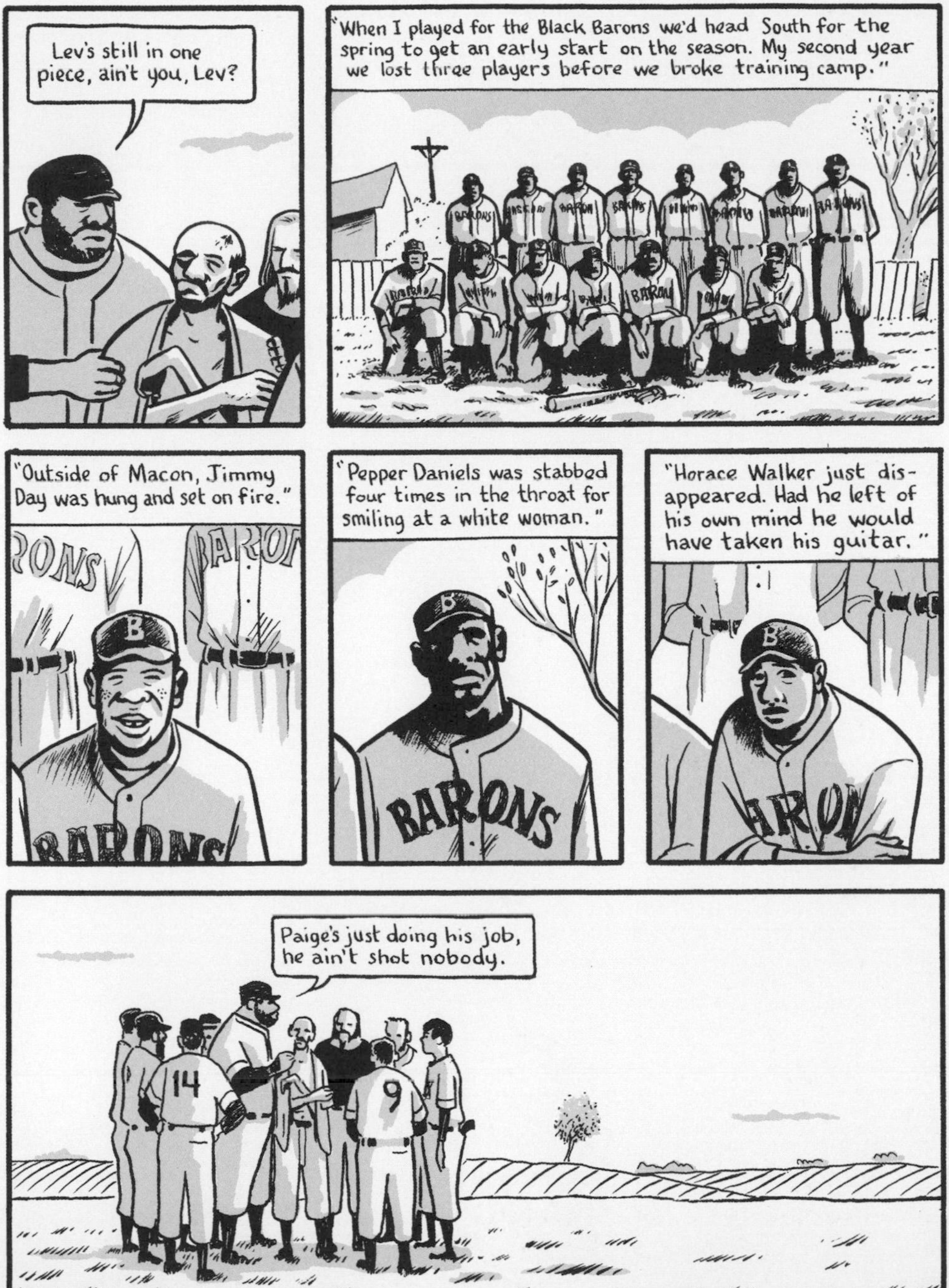

Lev's still in one piece, ain't you, Lev?
"When I played for the Black Barons we'd head South for the spring to get an early start on the season. My second year we lost three players before we broke training camp."
"Outside of Macon, Jimmy Day was hung and set on fire."
"Pepper Daniels was stabbed four times in the throat for smiling at a white woman."
"Horace Walker just dis-appeared. Had he left of his own mind he would have taken his guitar."
BARONS
Paige's just doing his job, he ain't shot nobody.
14
9

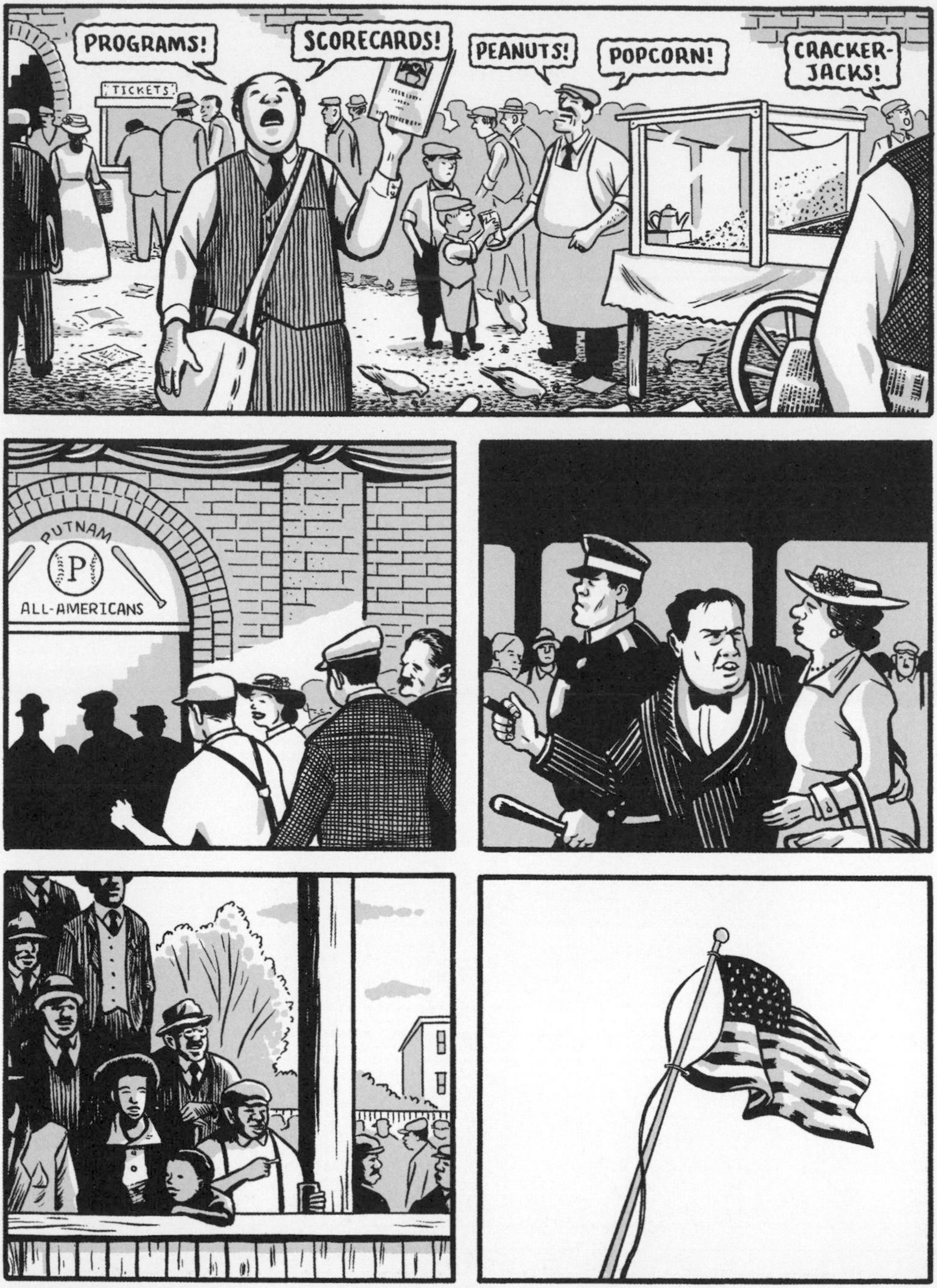
PROGRAMS!
SCORECARDS!
PEANUTS!
POPCORN!
CRACKER-JACKS!
TICKETS
PUTNAM
P
ALL-AMERICANS

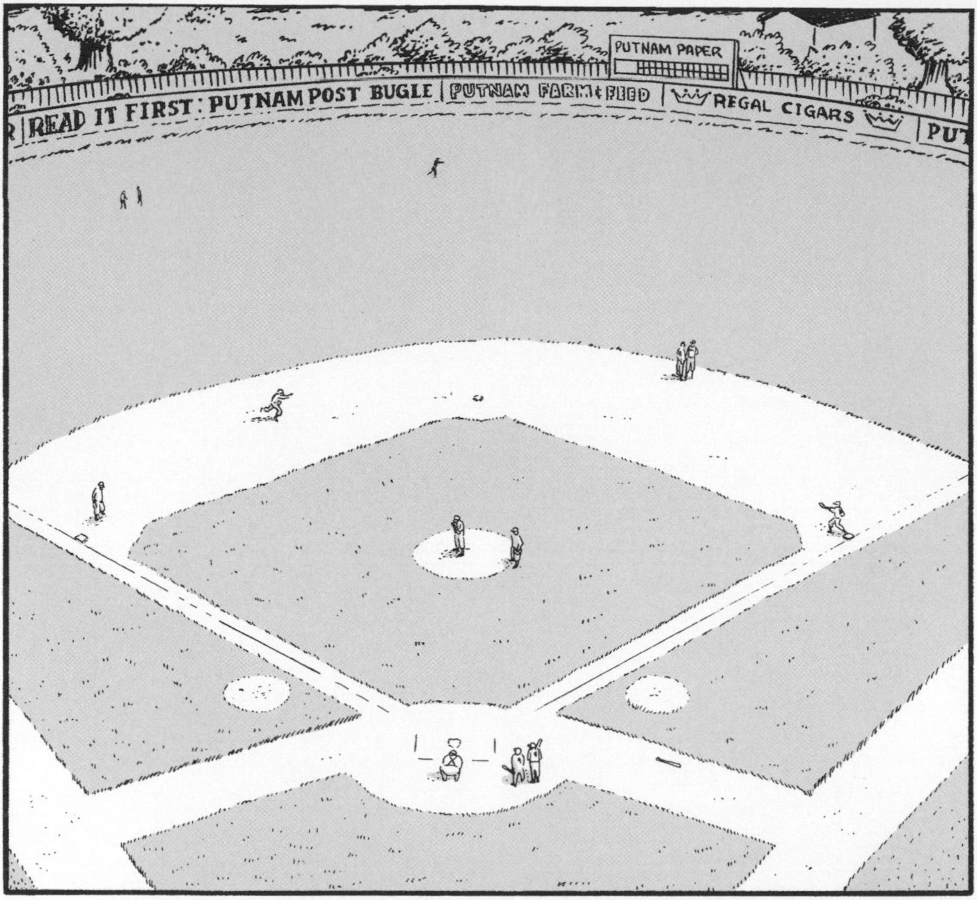
PUTNAM PAPER
READ IT FIRST: PUTNAM POST BUGLE
PUTNAM FARM & FEED
REGAL CIGARS
PUT

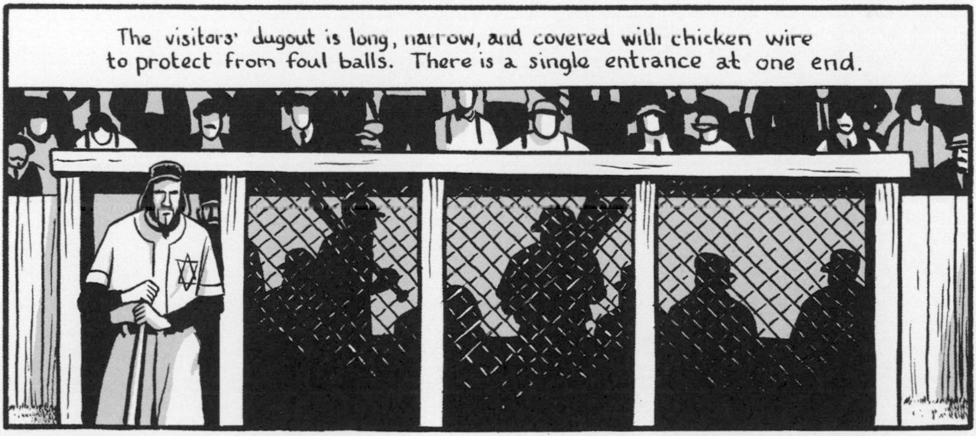
The visitors' dugout is long, narrow, and covered with chicken wire to protect from foul balls. There is a single entrance at one end.

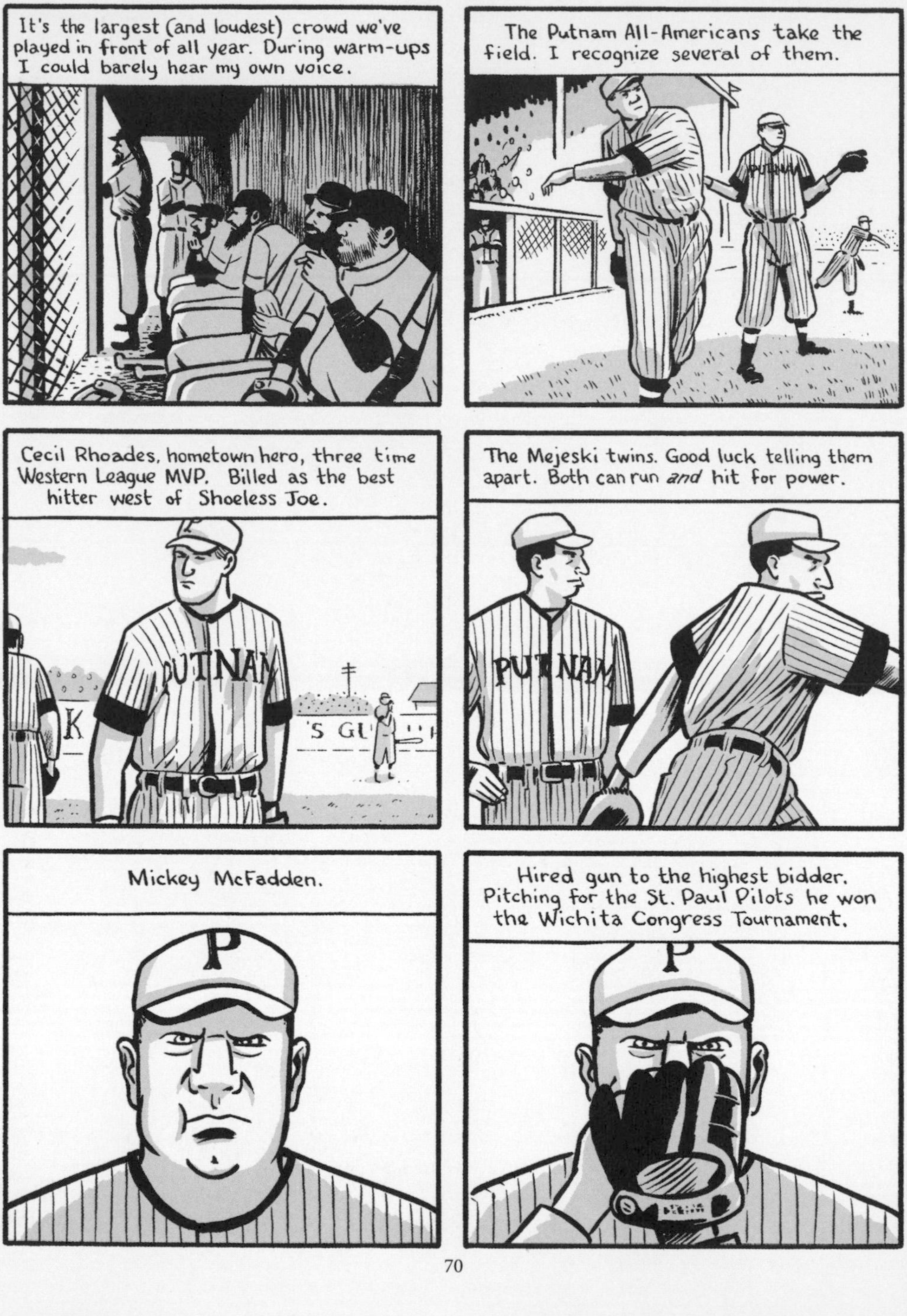

It's the largest (and loudest) crowd we've played in front of all year. During warm-ups I could barely hear my own voice.
The Putnam All-Americans take the field. I recognize several of them.
Cecil Rhoades, hometown hero, three time Western League MVP. Billed as the best hitter west of Shoeless Joe.
The Mejeski twins. Good luck telling them apart. Both can run *and* hit for power.
Mickey McFadden.
Hired gun to the highest bidder. Pitching for the St. Paul Pilots he won the Wichita Congress Tournament.

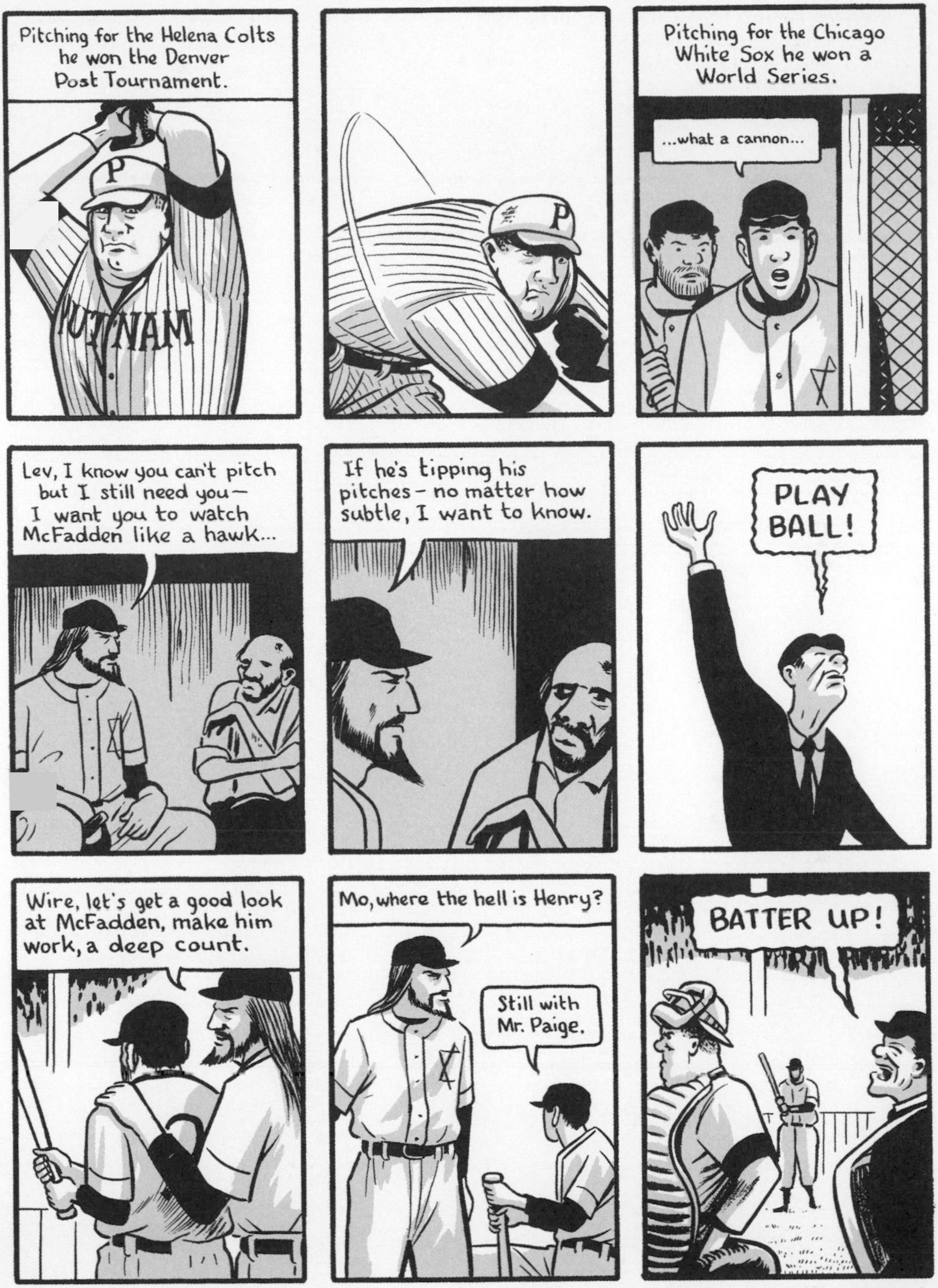
Pitching for the Helena Colts he won the Denver Post Tournament.
PUTNAM
Pitching for the Chicago White Sox he won a World Series.
...what a cannon...
Lev, I know you can't pitch but I still need you— I want you to watch McFadden like a hawk...
If he's tipping his pitches— no matter how subtle, I want to know.
PLAY BALL!
Wire, let's get a good look at McFadden, make him work, a deep count.
Mo, where the hell is Henry?
Still with Mr. Paige.
BATTER UP!

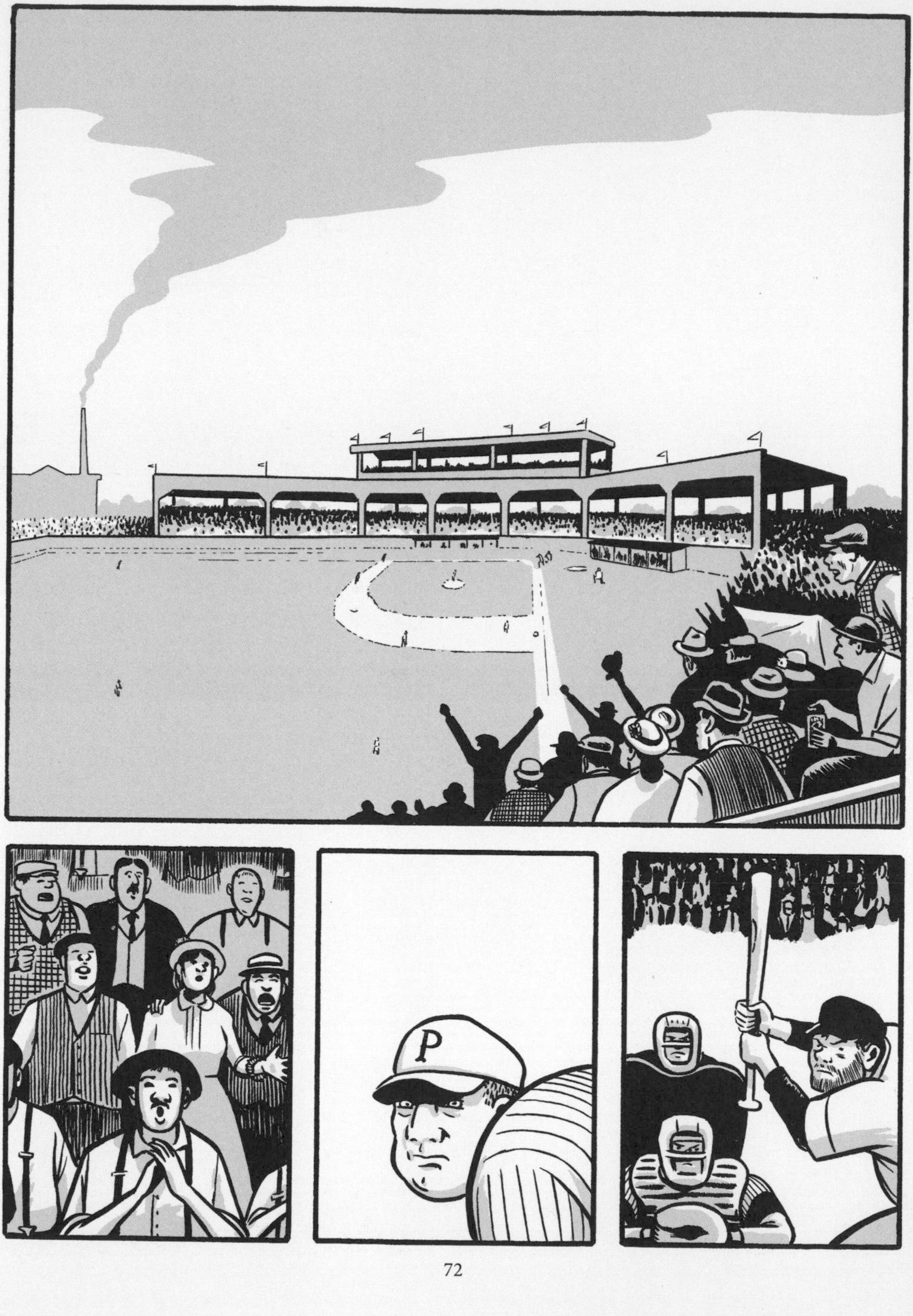

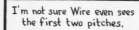

STRIKE ONE!

I'm not sure Wire even sees the first two pitches.

STRIKE TWO!

Wire steps out of the box as the crowd grows louder, anticipating a strikeout.

McFadden wastes a pitch high. Wire doesn't chase. 1 and 2.

Next pitch is inside heat. Wire fouls it off (barely).

Fooled badly on a vicious breaking ball. Strike three.

So much for a deep count. Mo steps tentatively towards the batter's box.

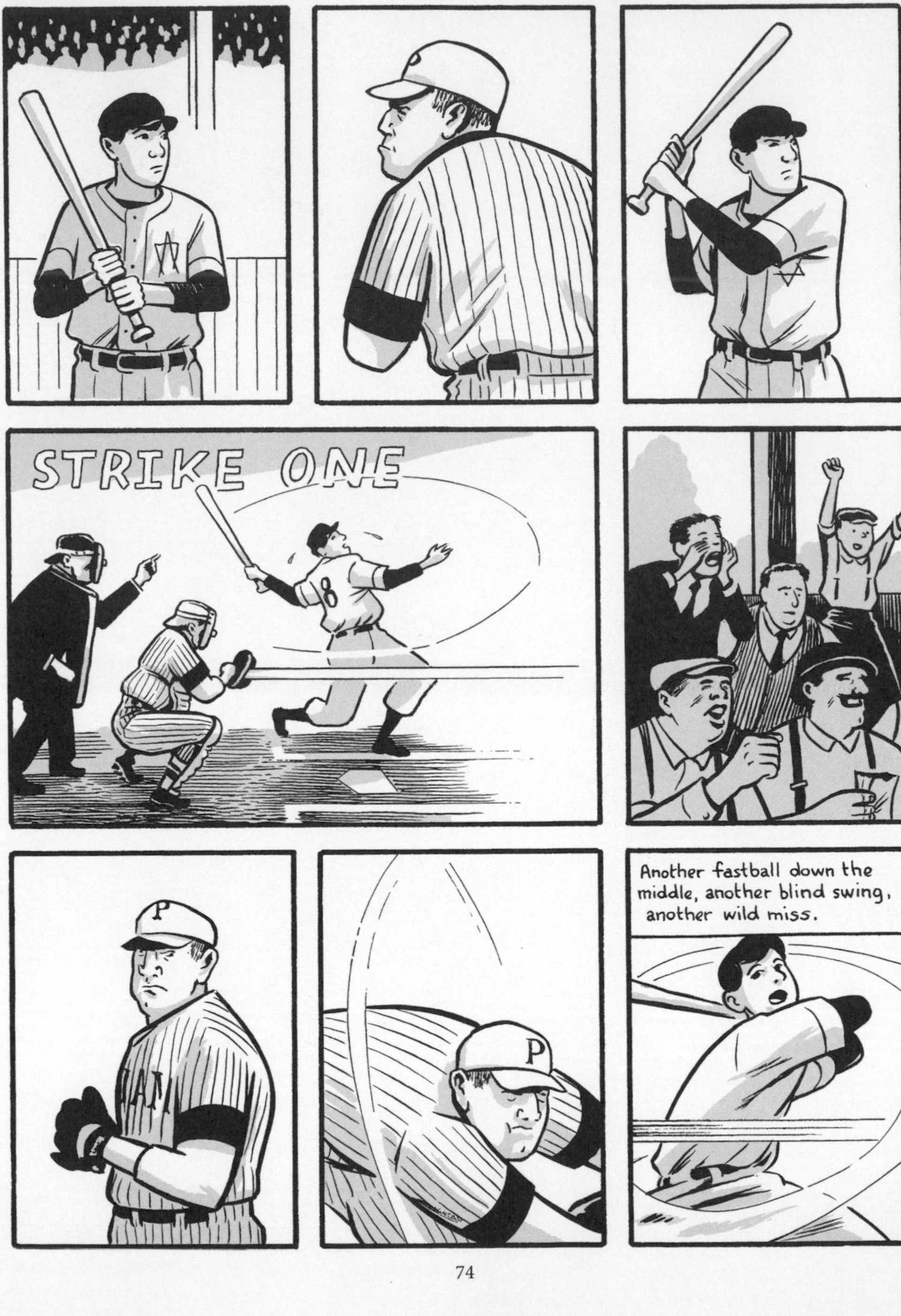
STRIKE ONE
Another fastball down the middle, another blind swing, another wild miss.

PUTNAM

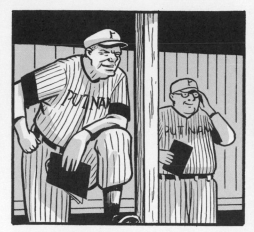

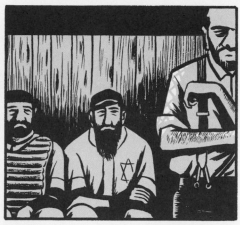

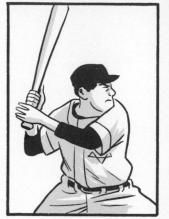

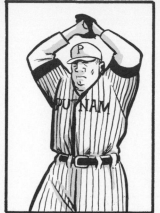

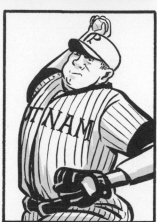

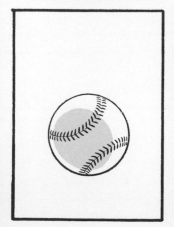

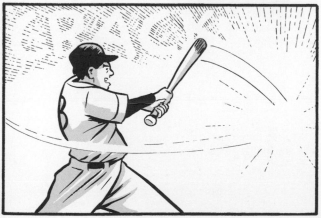

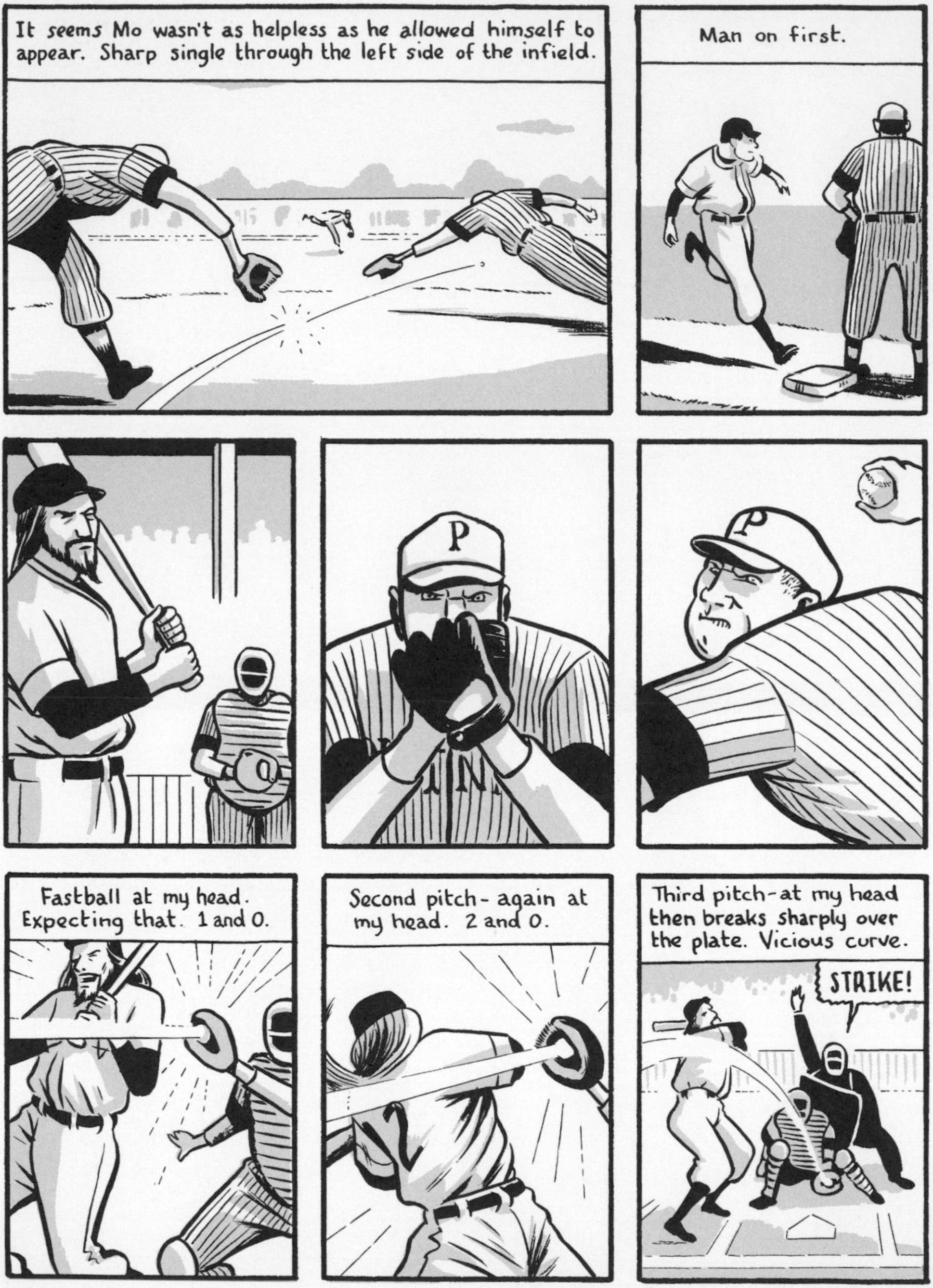
It seems Mo wasn't as helpless as he allowed himself to appear. Sharp single through the left side of the infield.
Man on first.
Fastball at my head. Expecting that. 1 and 0.
Second pitch- again at my head. 2 and 0.
Third pitch-at my head then breaks sharply over the plate. Vicious curve.
STRIKE!

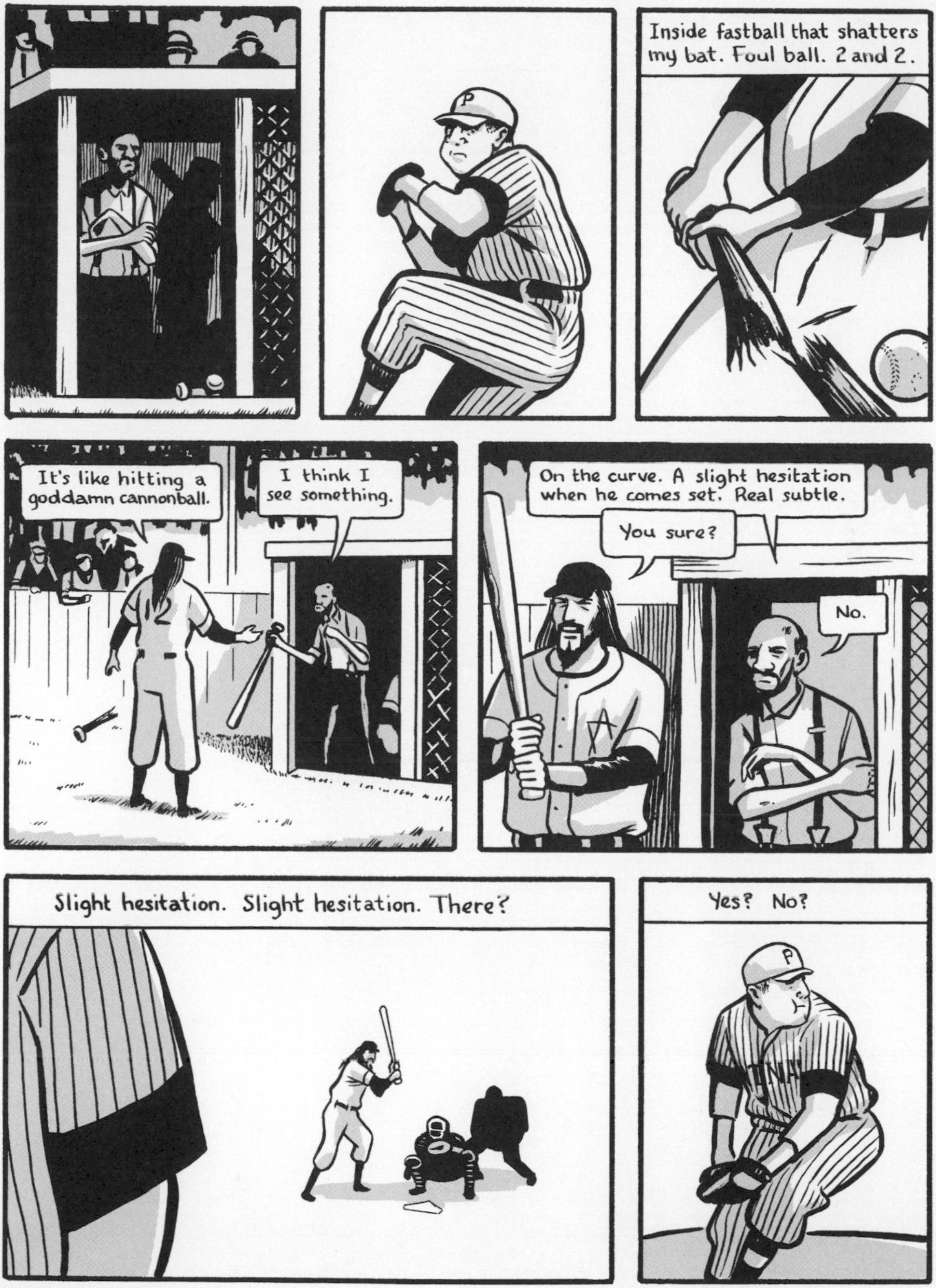
Inside fastball that shatters my bat. Foul ball. 2 and 2.
It's like hitting a goddamn cannonball.
I think I see something.
On the curve. A slight hesitation when he comes set. Real subtle.
You sure?
No.
Slight hesitation. Slight hesitation. There?
Yes? No?

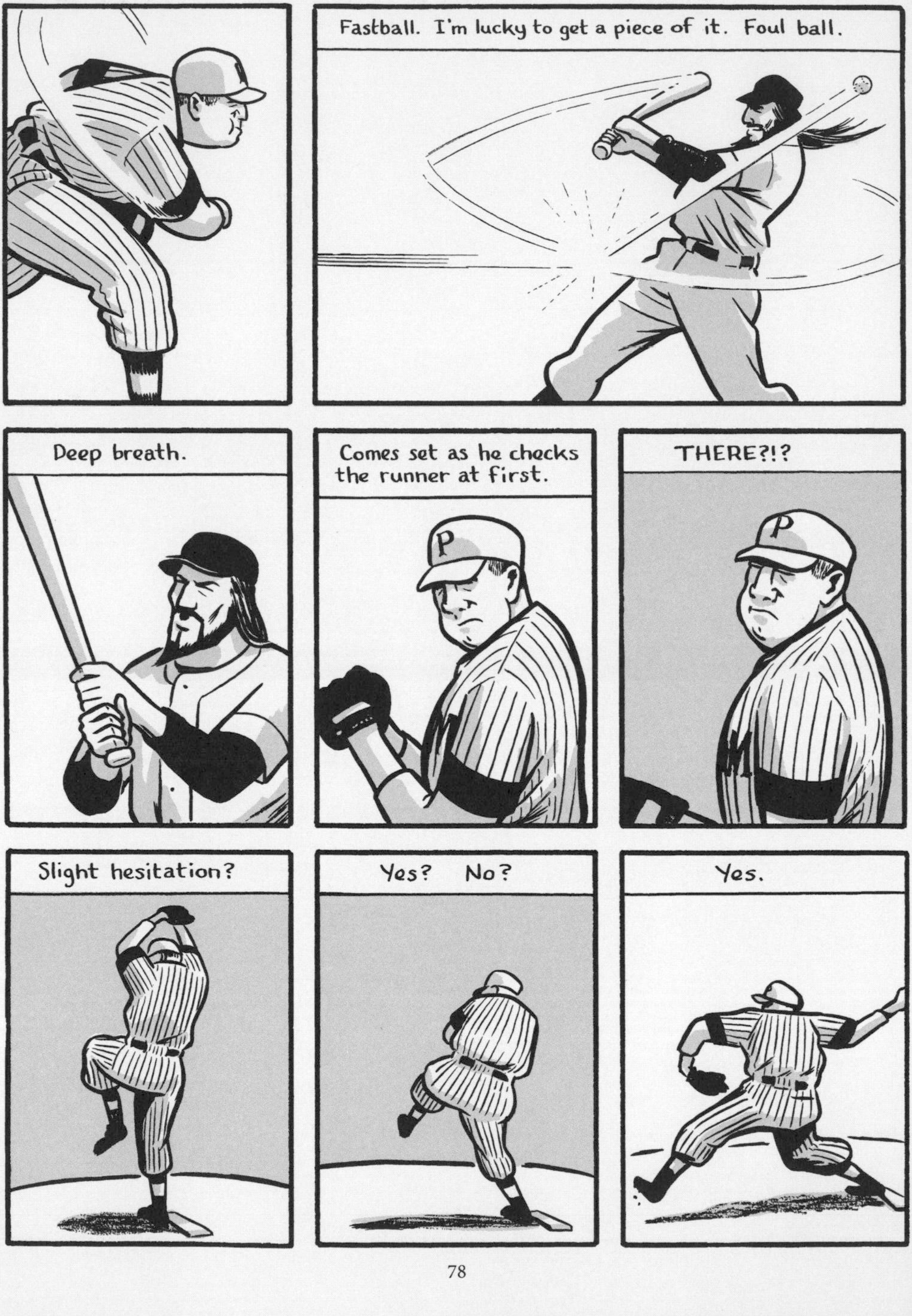
Fastball. I'm lucky to get a piece of it. Foul ball.
Deep breath.
Comes set as he checks the runner at first.
THERE?!?
Slight hesitation?
Yes? No?
Yes.

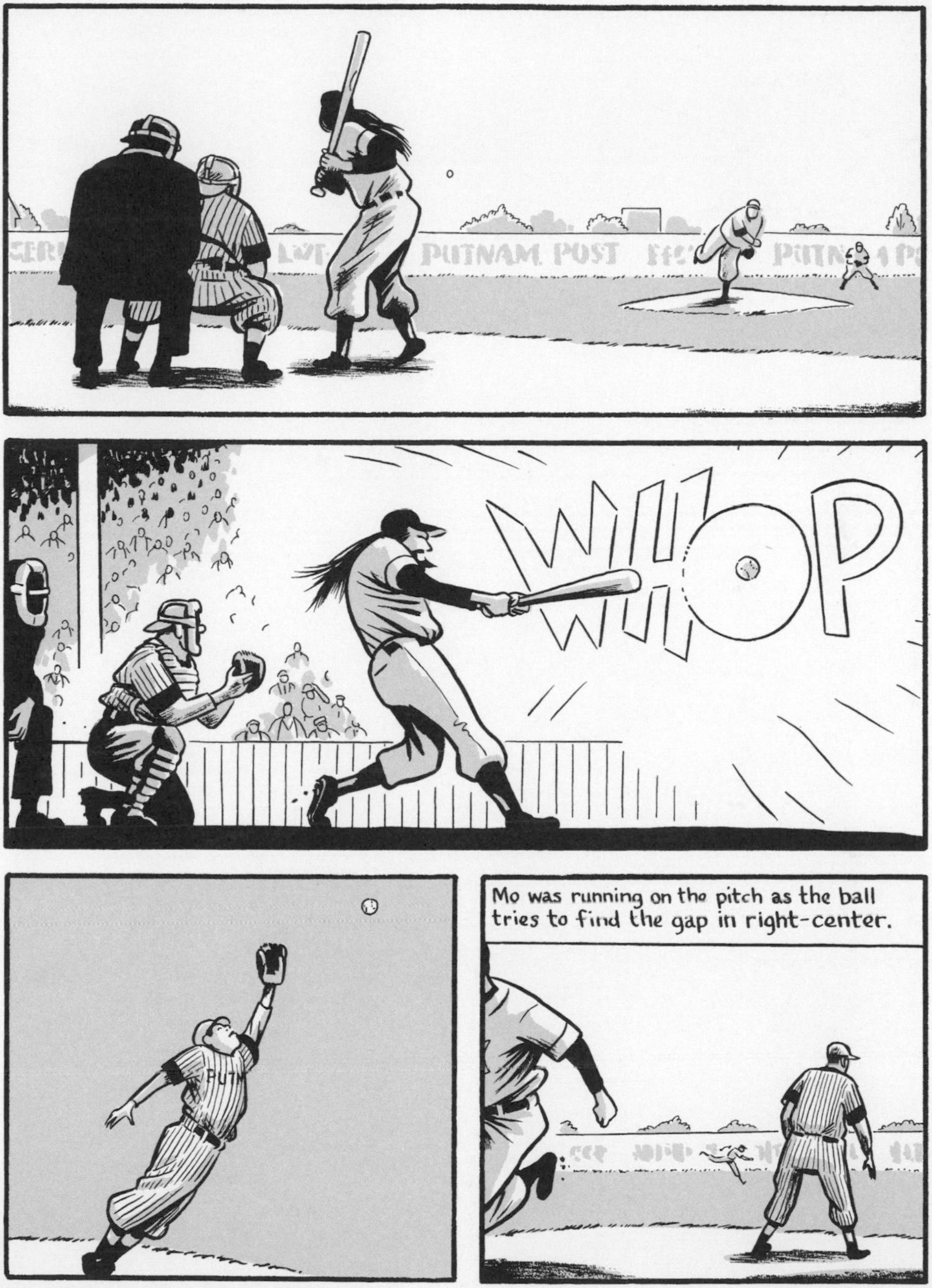
PUTNAM POST
WHOP
Mo was running on the pitch as the ball tries to find the gap in right-center.

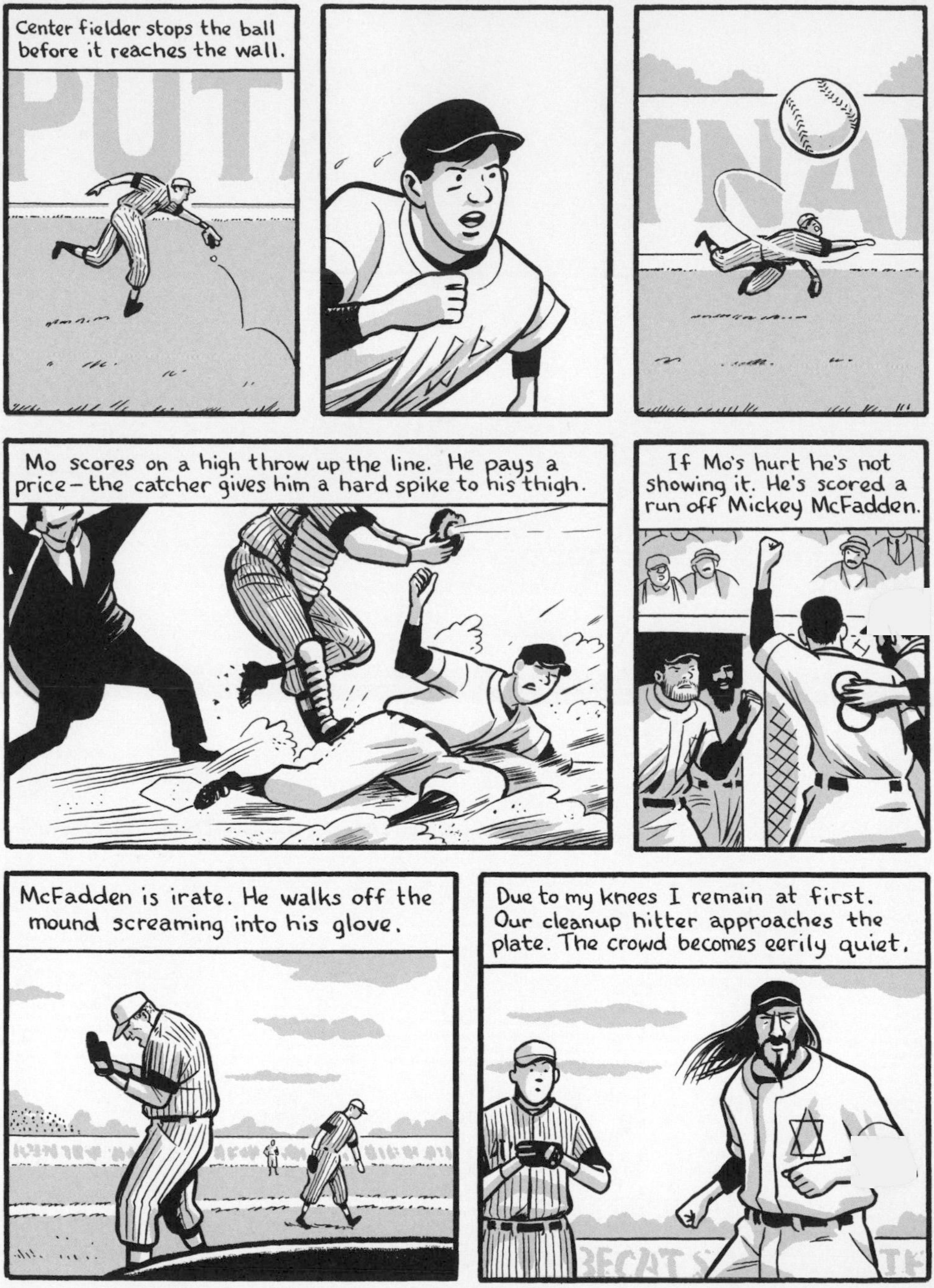
Center fielder stops the ball before it reaches the wall.
PUT
TNA
Mo scores on a high throw up the line. He pays a price – the catcher gives him a hard spike to his thigh.
If Mo's hurt he's not showing it. He's scored a run off Mickey McFadden.
McFadden is irate. He walks off the mound screaming into his glove.
Due to my knees I remain at first. Our cleanup hitter approaches the plate. The crowd becomes eerily quiet.

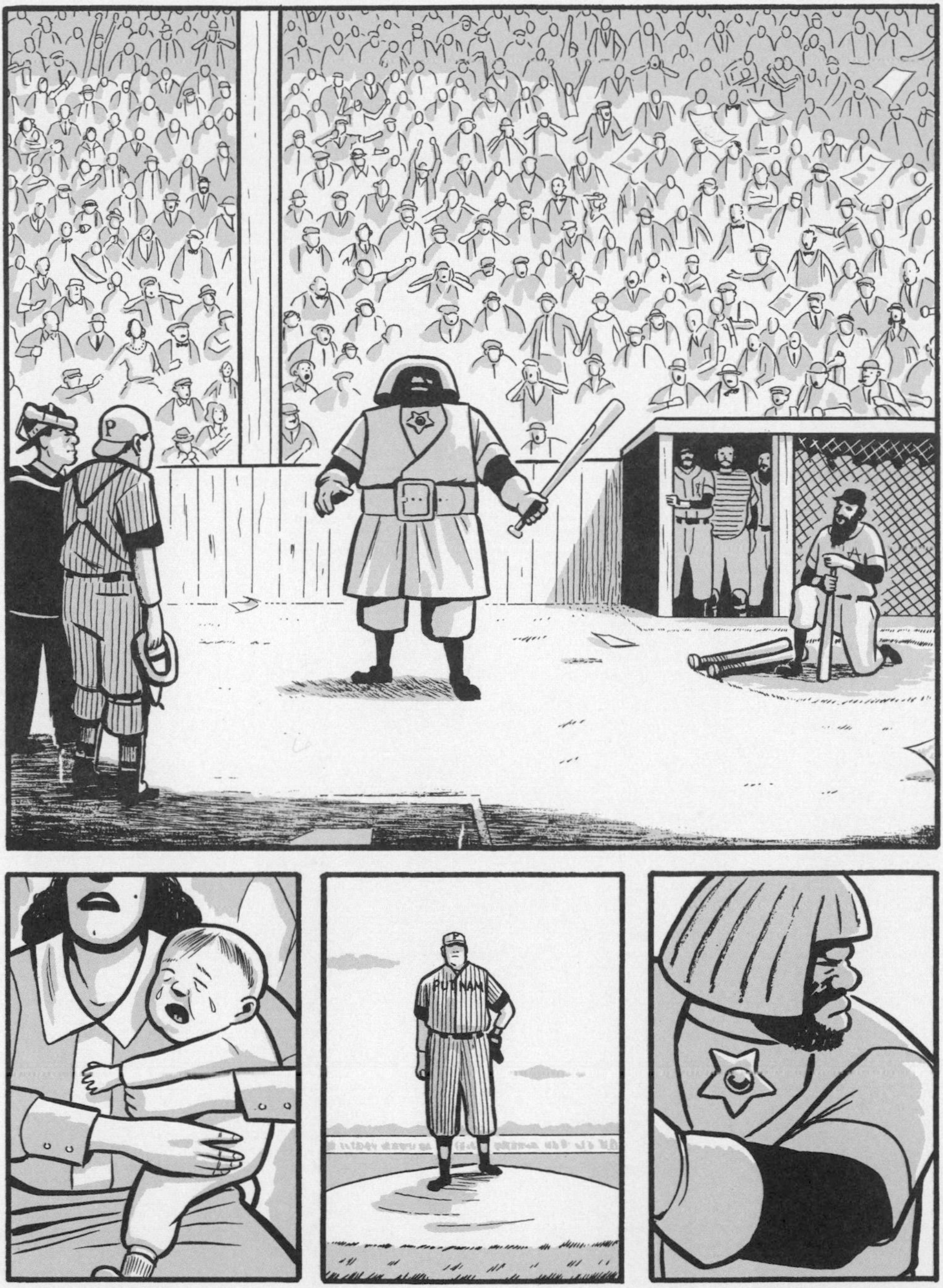

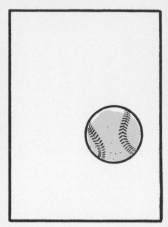

A squib, right back to the mound.

McFadden fires to second.

Second to first.

Double play. Inning over.

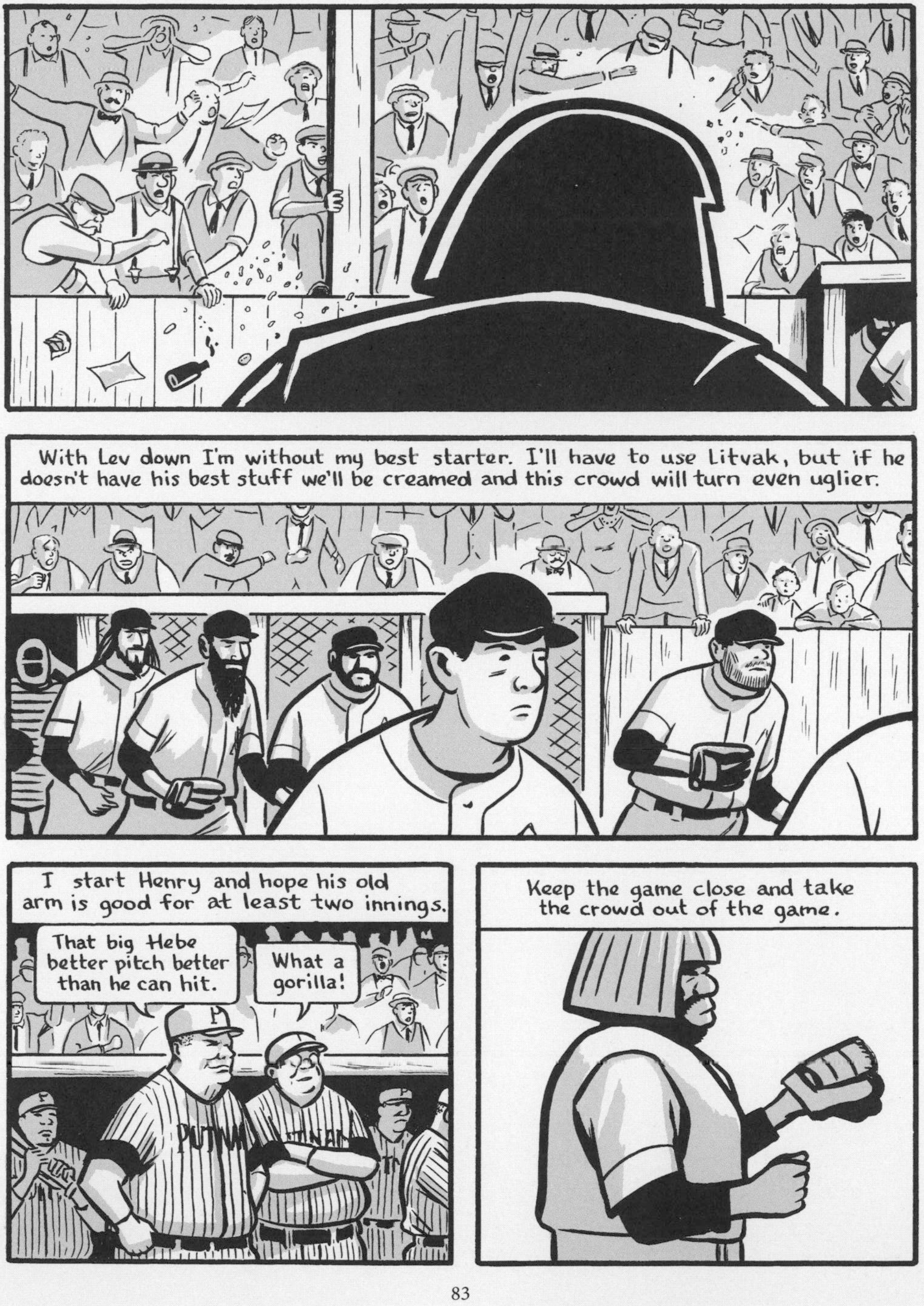
With Lev down I'm without my best starter. I'll have to use Litvak, but if he doesn't have his best stuff we'll be creamed and this crowd will turn even uglier.
I start Henry and hope his old arm is good for at least two innings.
That big Hebe better pitch better than he can hit.
What a gorilla!
Keep the game close and take the crowd out of the game.

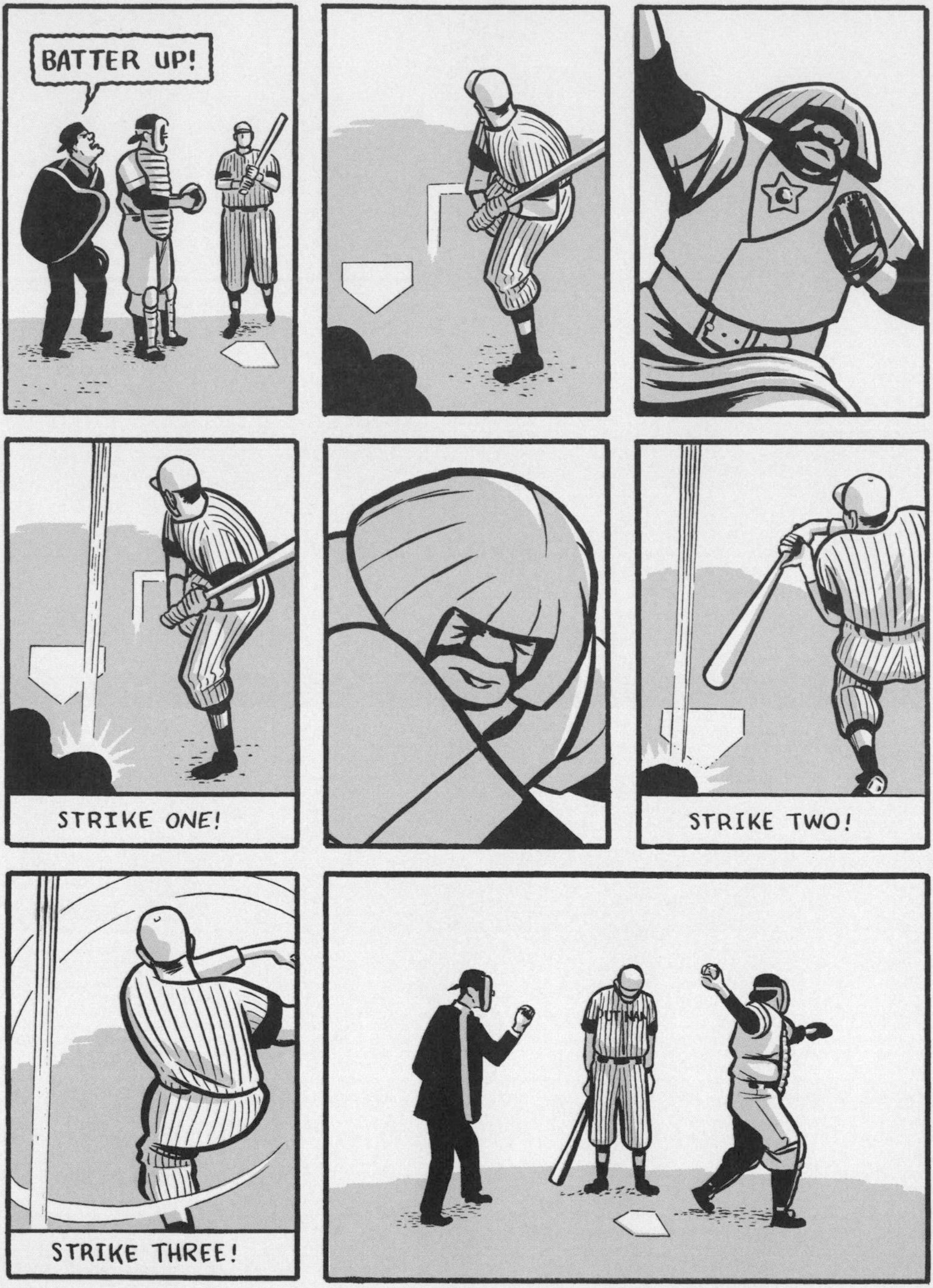
BATTER UP!
STRIKE ONE!
STRIKE TWO!
STRIKE THREE!

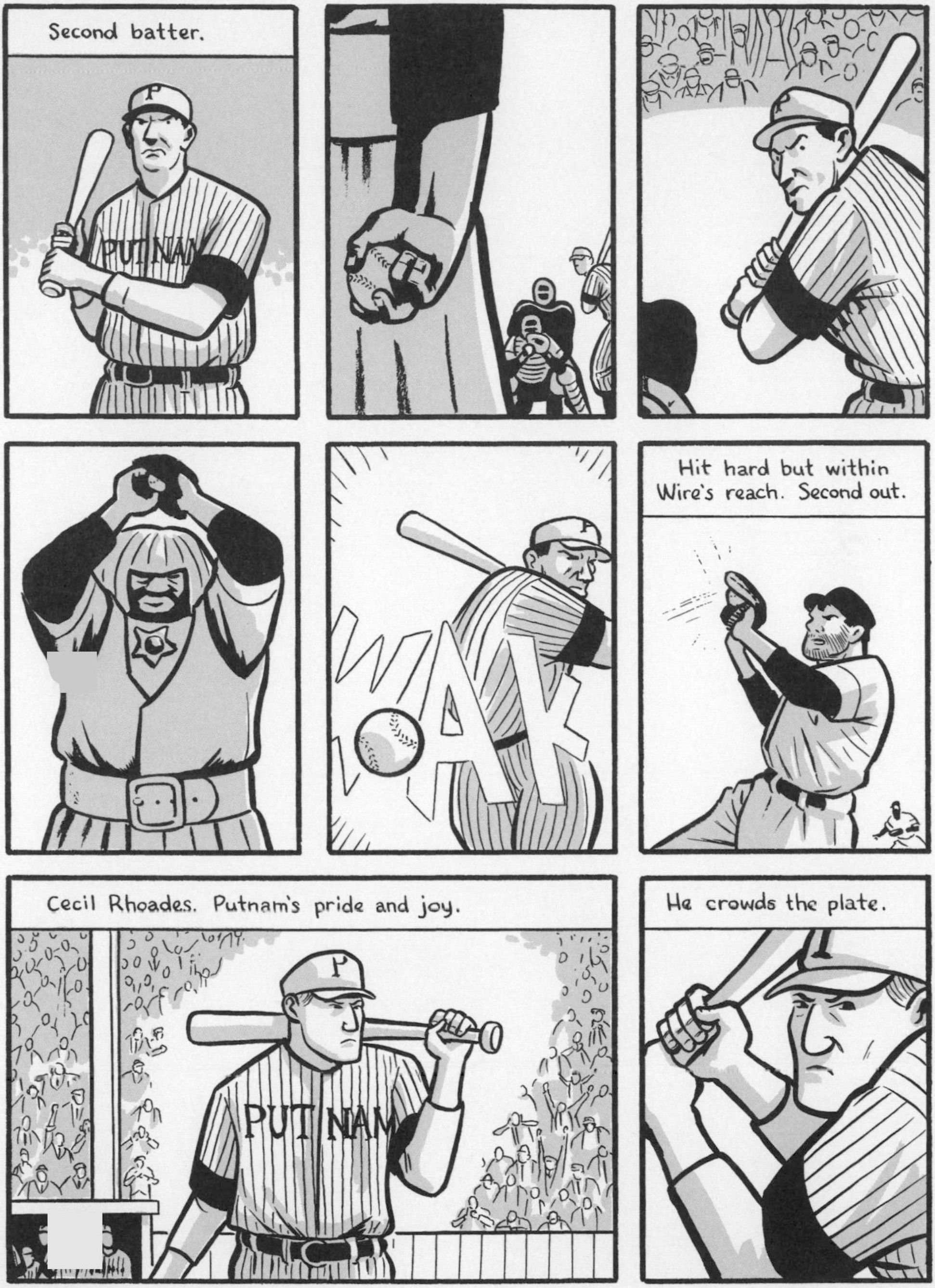
Second batter.
PUTNAM
WAK
Hit hard but within Wire's reach. Second out.
Cecil Rhoades. Putnam's pride and joy.
PUTNAM
He crowds the plate.

The first pitch—in tight, inches from Rhoades's chin. Doesn't even flinch. 1 and 0.

Another inside fastball is called for.

Go on, get out of here...

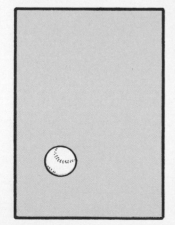

Four hundred footer, but pulled foul. 1 and 1.

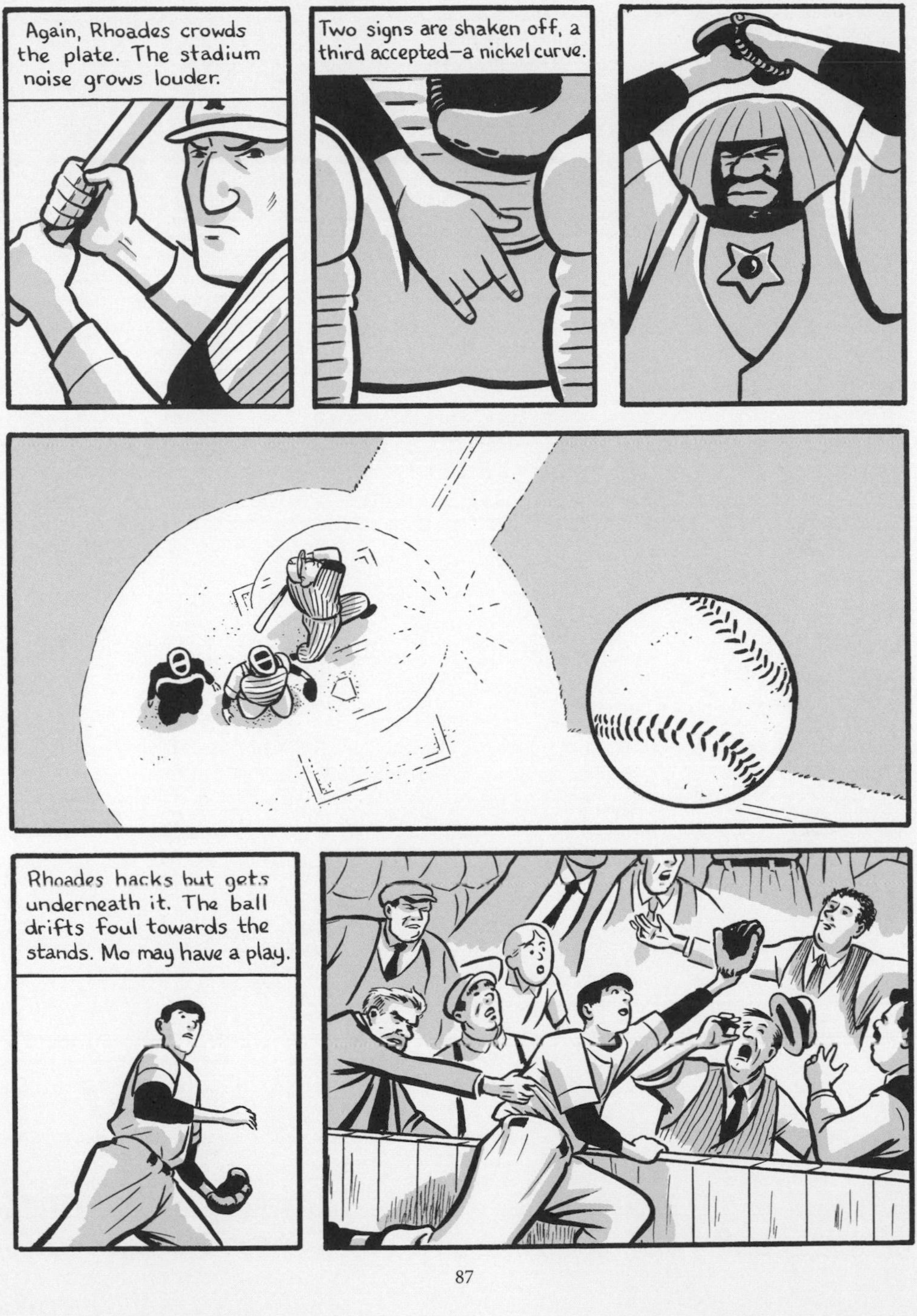
Again, Rhoades crowds the plate. The stadium noise grows louder.
Two signs are shaken off, a third accepted—a nickel curve.
Rhoades hacks but gets underneath it. The ball drifts foul towards the stands. Mo may have a play.

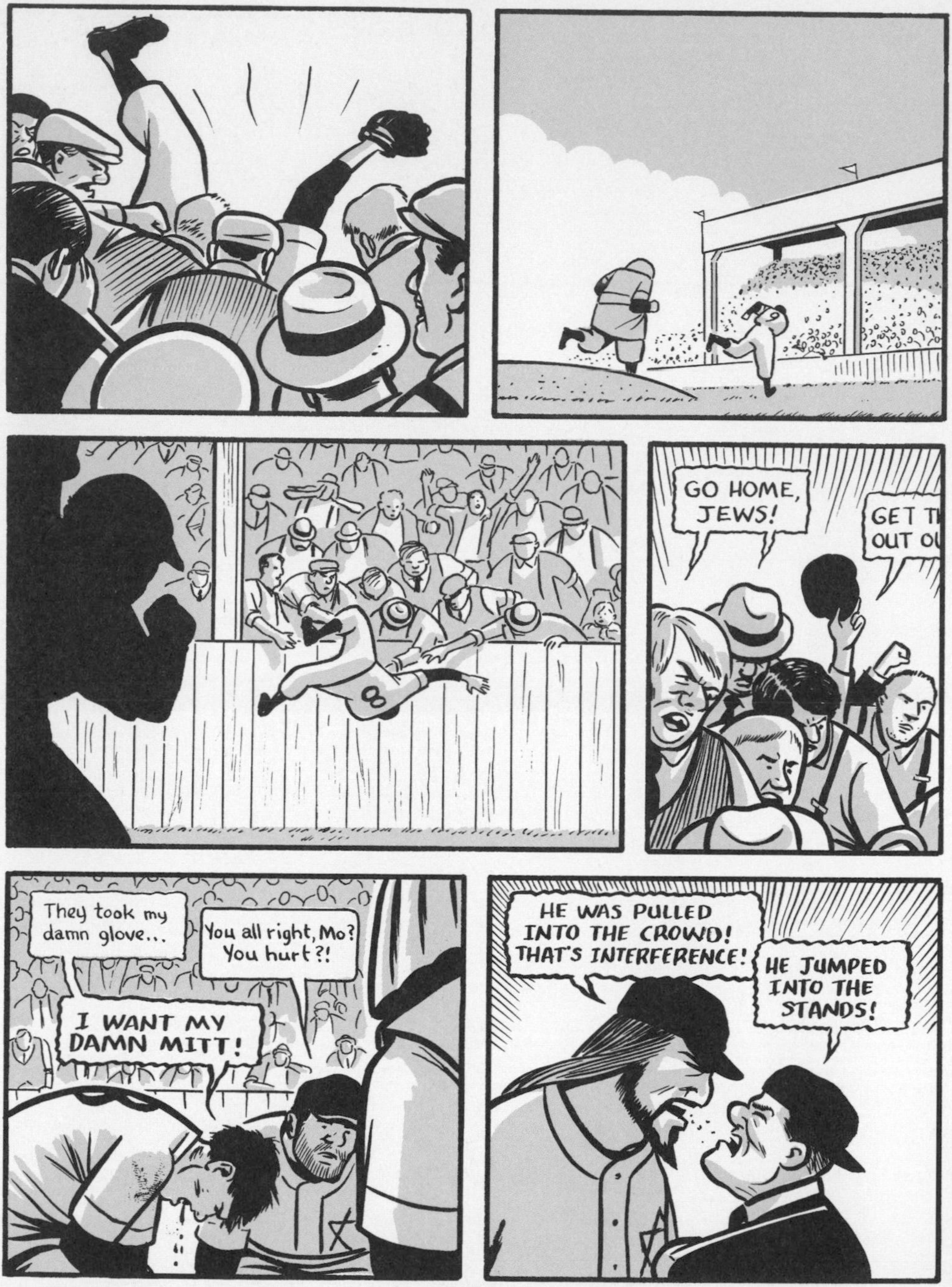
GO HOME, JEWS!
GET TH
OUT OU
They took my damn glove...
You all right, Mo? You hurt?!
I WANT MY DAMN MITT!
HE WAS PULLED INTO THE CROWD! THAT'S INTERFERENCE!
HE JUMPED INTO THE STANDS!

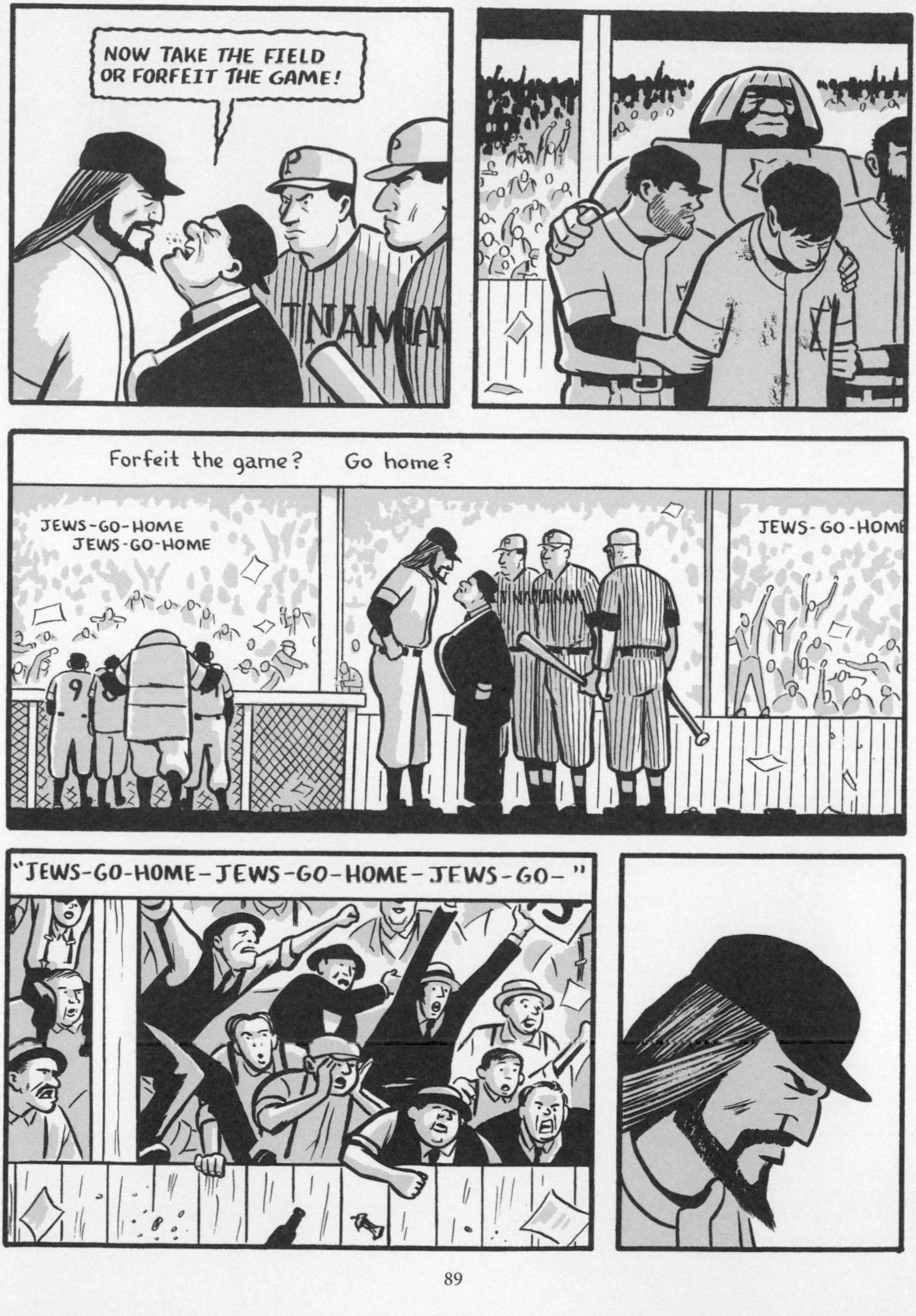
NOW TAKE THE FIELD OR FORFEIT THE GAME!
Forfeit the game? Go home?
JEWS-GO-HOME
JEWS-GO-HOME
JEWS-GO-HOME
"JEWS-GO-HOME-JEWS-GO-HOME-JEWS-GO-"

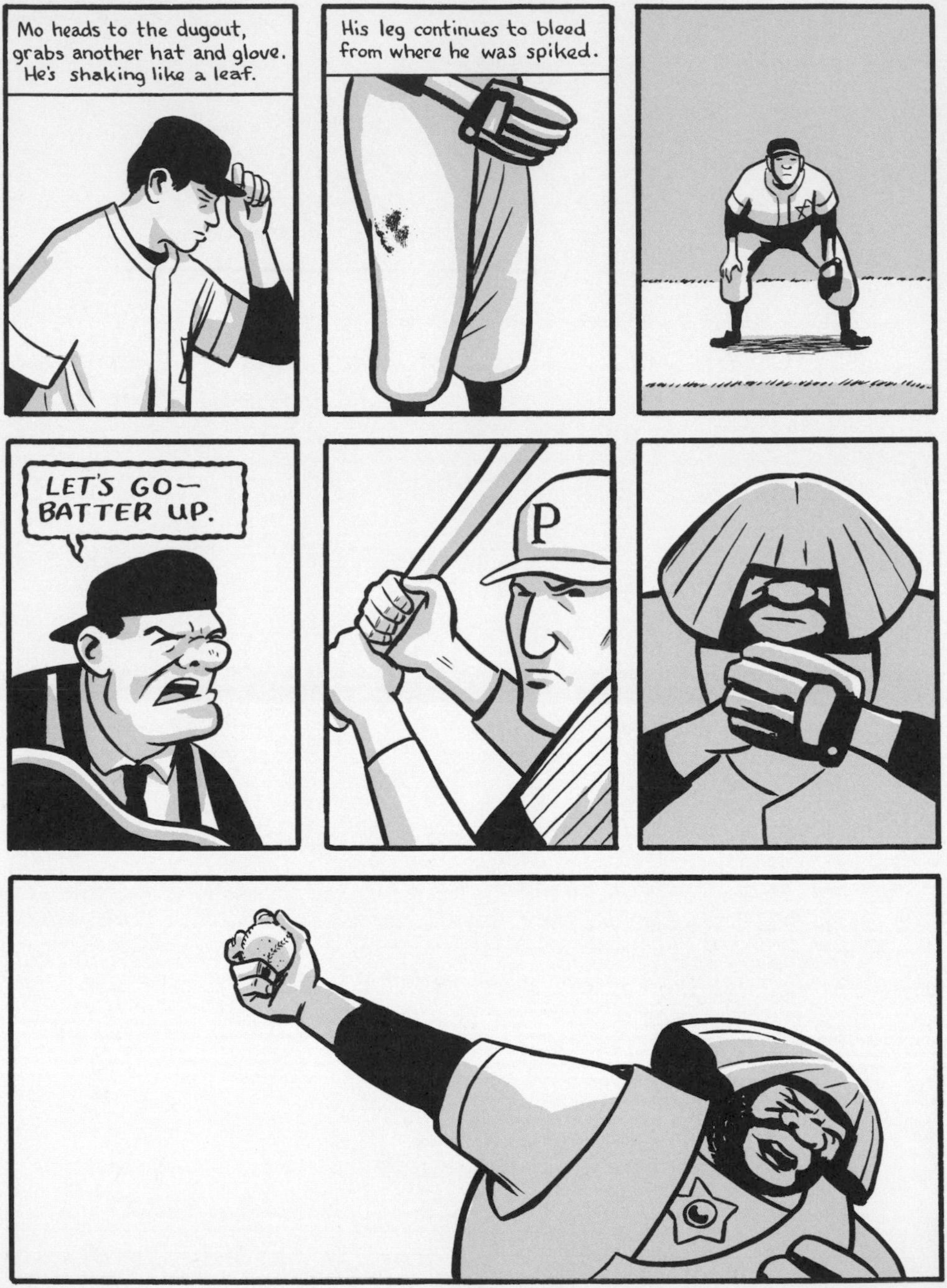
Mo heads to the dugout, grabs another hat and glove. He's shaking like a leaf.
His leg continues to bleed from where he was spiked.
LET'S GO— BATTER UP.
P

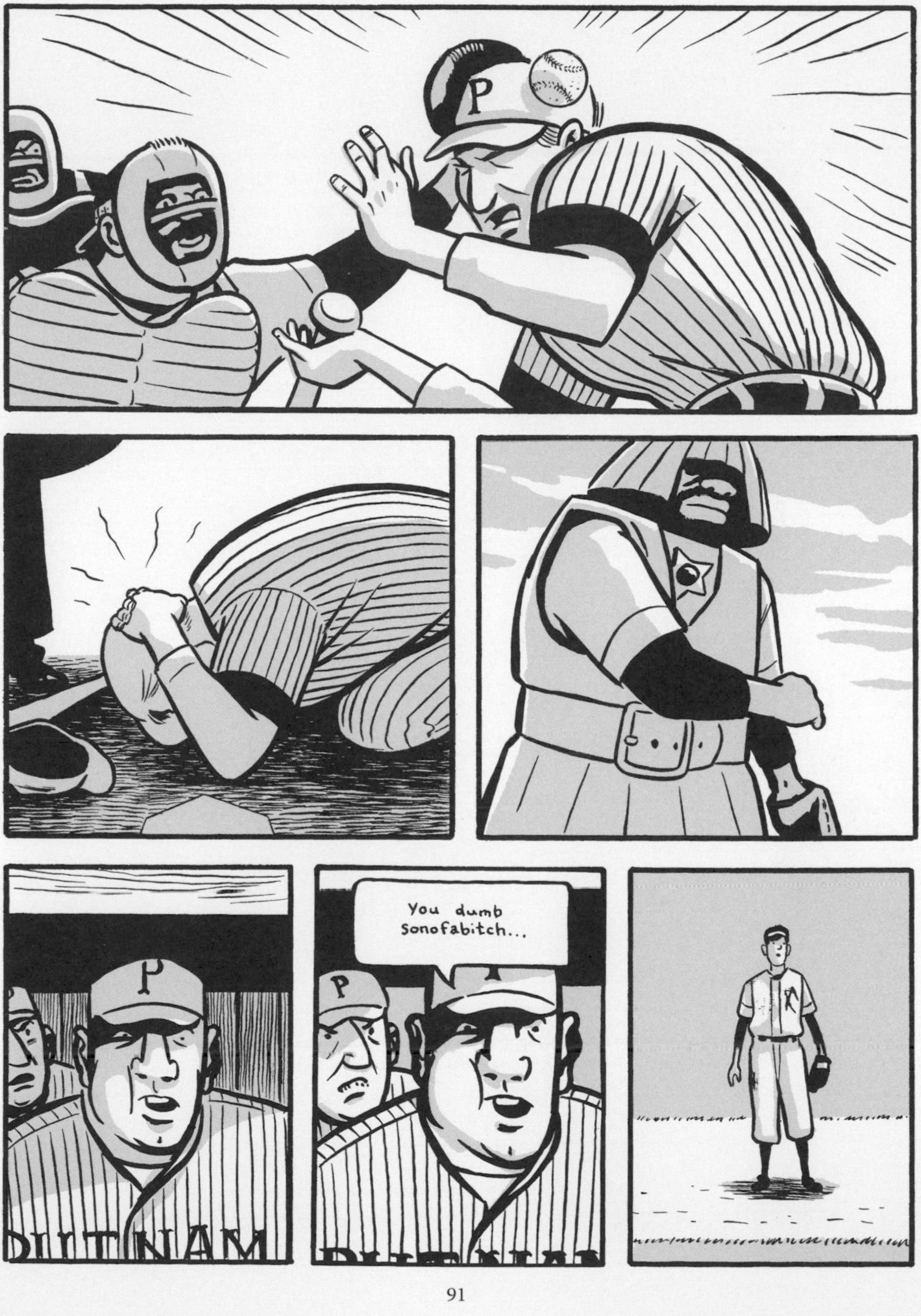
You dumb sonofabitch...

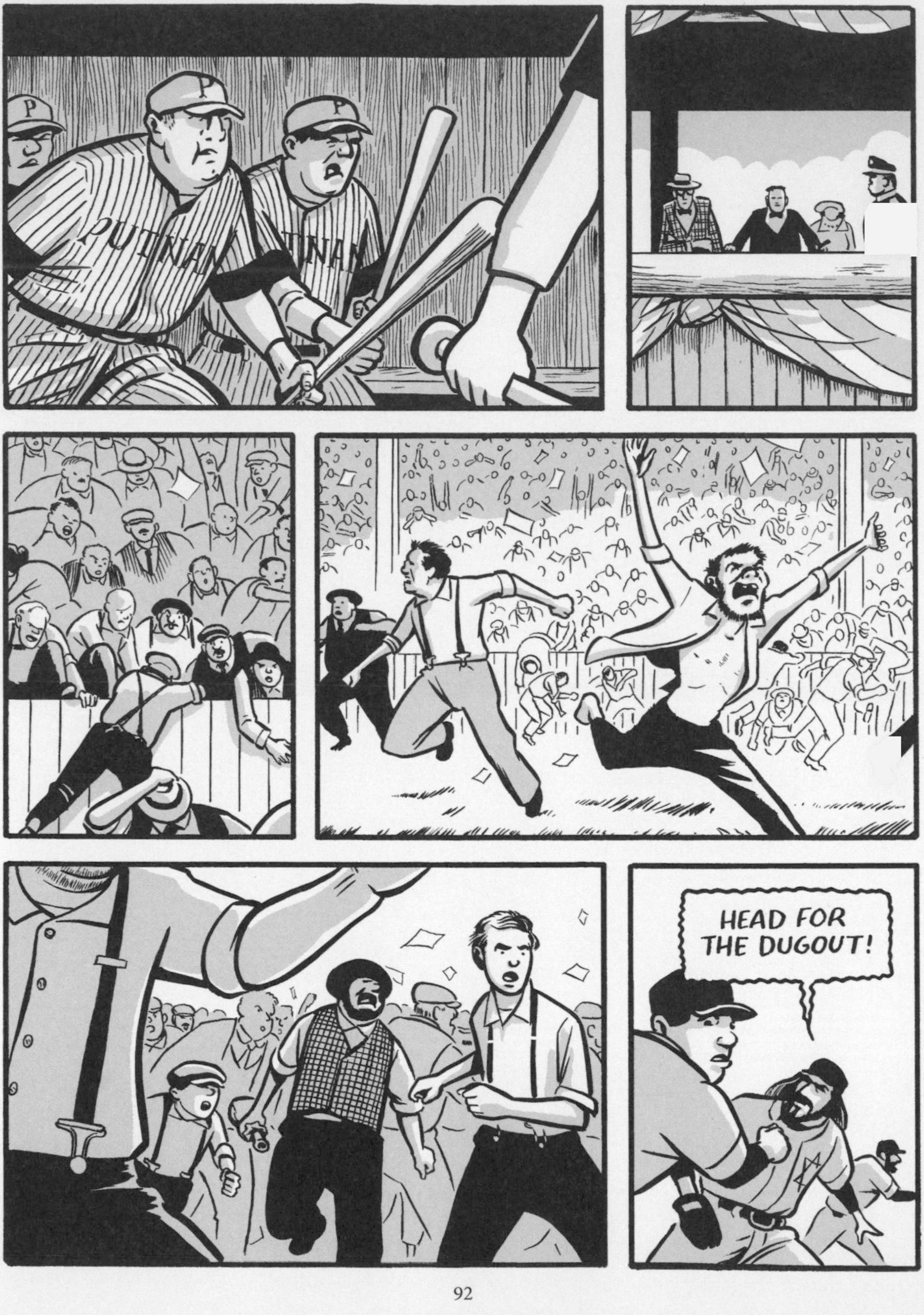
PUTNAM
PUTNAM
HEAD FOR THE DUGOUT!

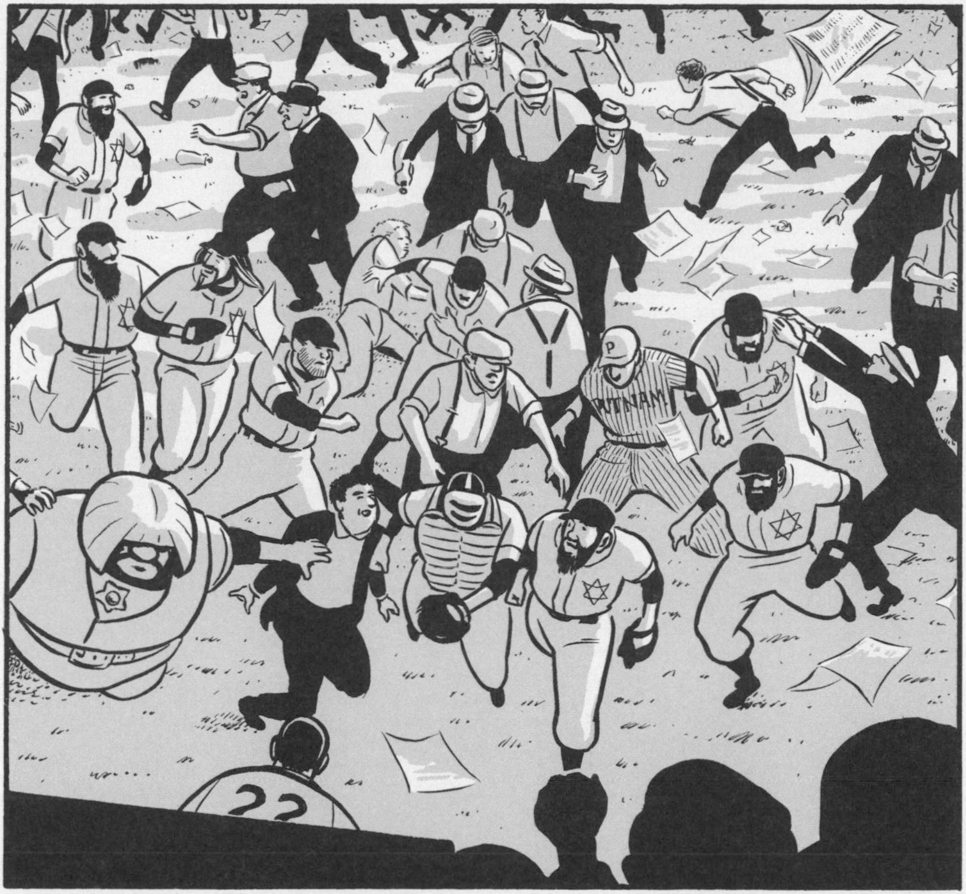
PUTNAM
22

Somehow we make it to the dugout intact. As the crowd bears down, Henry attempts to protect the dugout's single entrance.

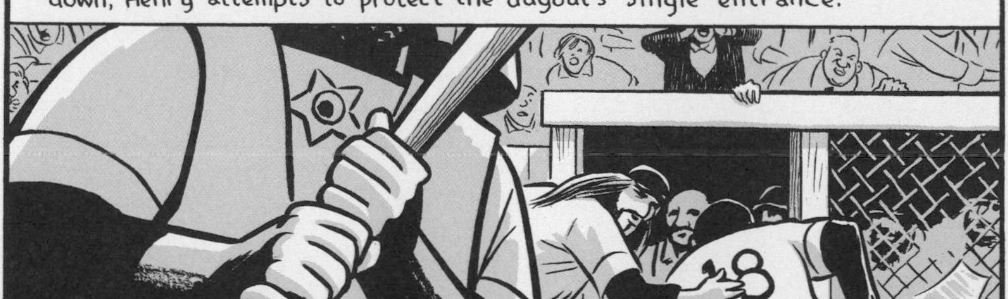
18

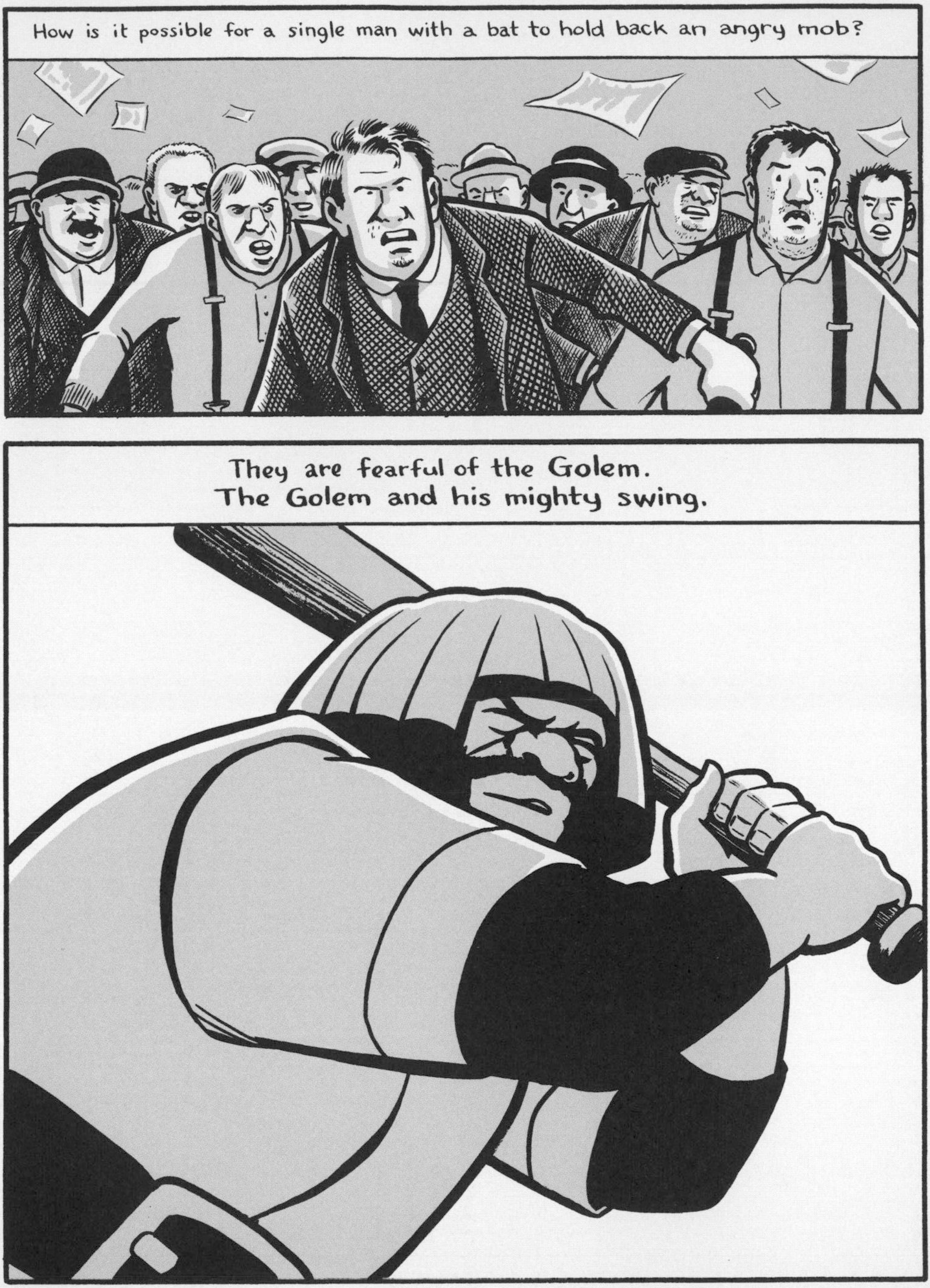
How is it possible for a single man with a bat to hold back an angry mob?
They are fearful of the Golem.
The Golem and his mighty swing.

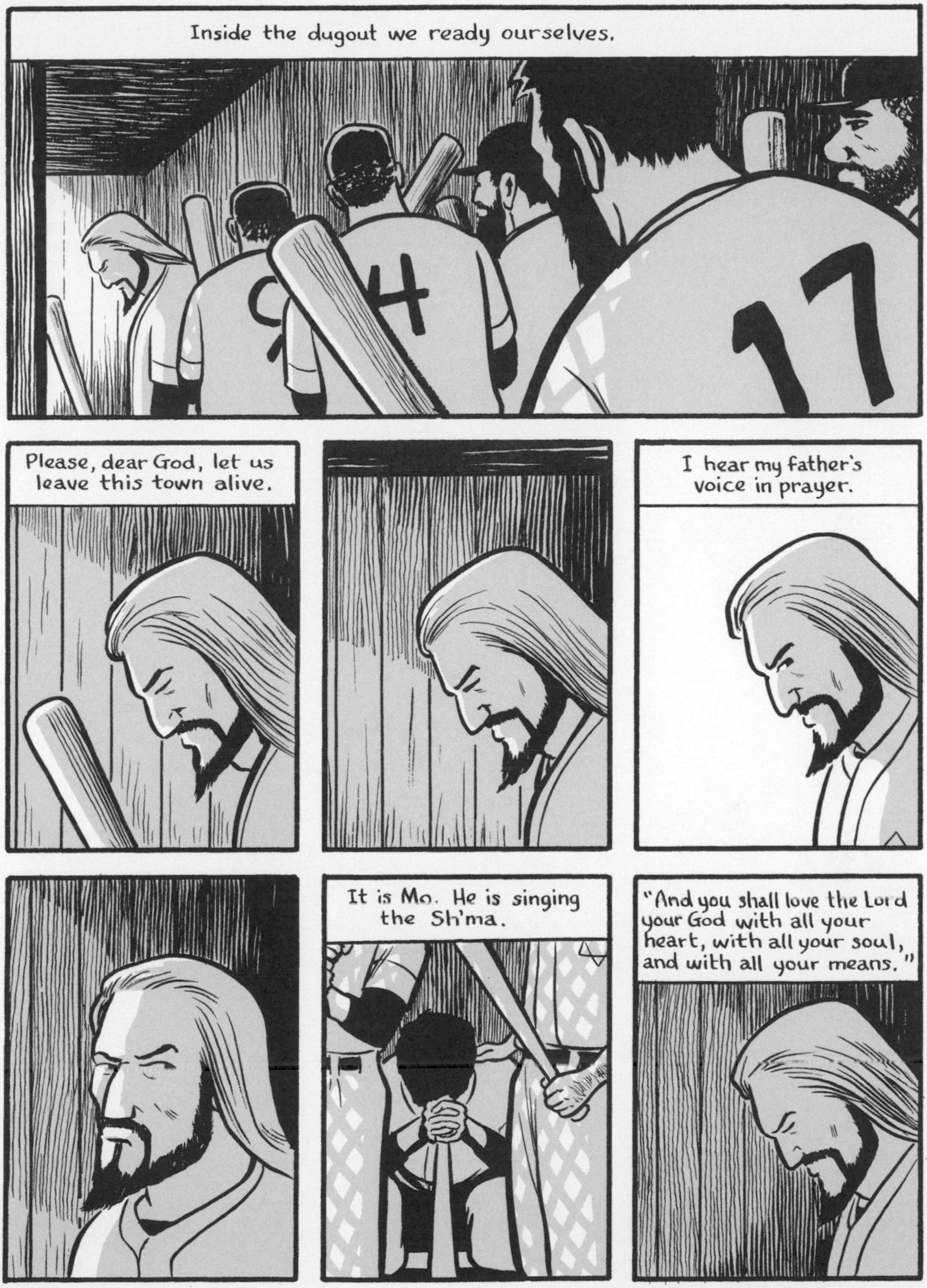
Inside the dugout we ready ourselves.
Please, dear God, let us leave this town alive.
I hear my father's voice in prayer.
It is Mo. He is singing the Sh'ma.
"And you shall love the Lord your God with all your heart, with all your soul, and with all your means."

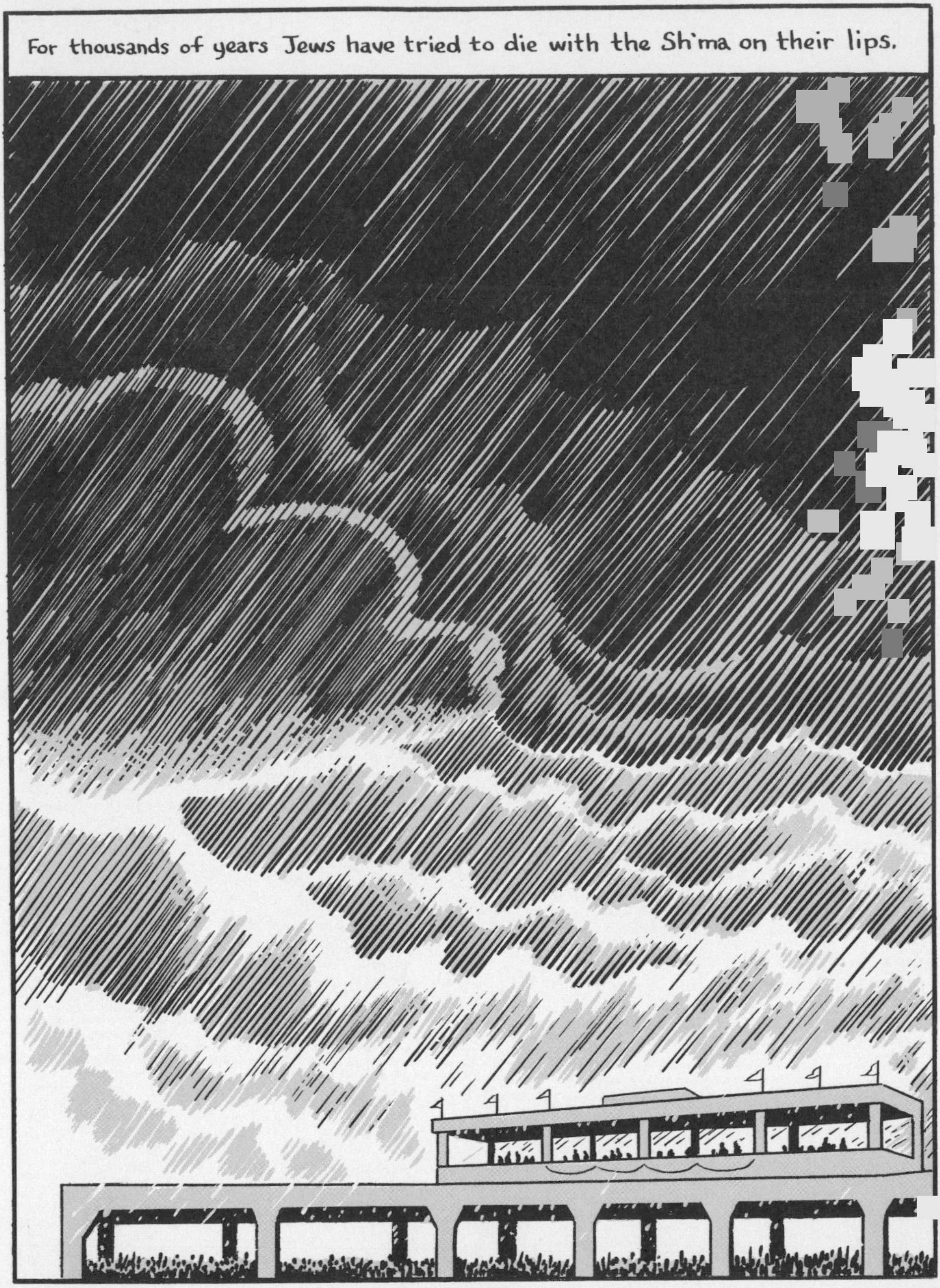
For thousands of years Jews have tried to die with the Sh'ma on their lips.

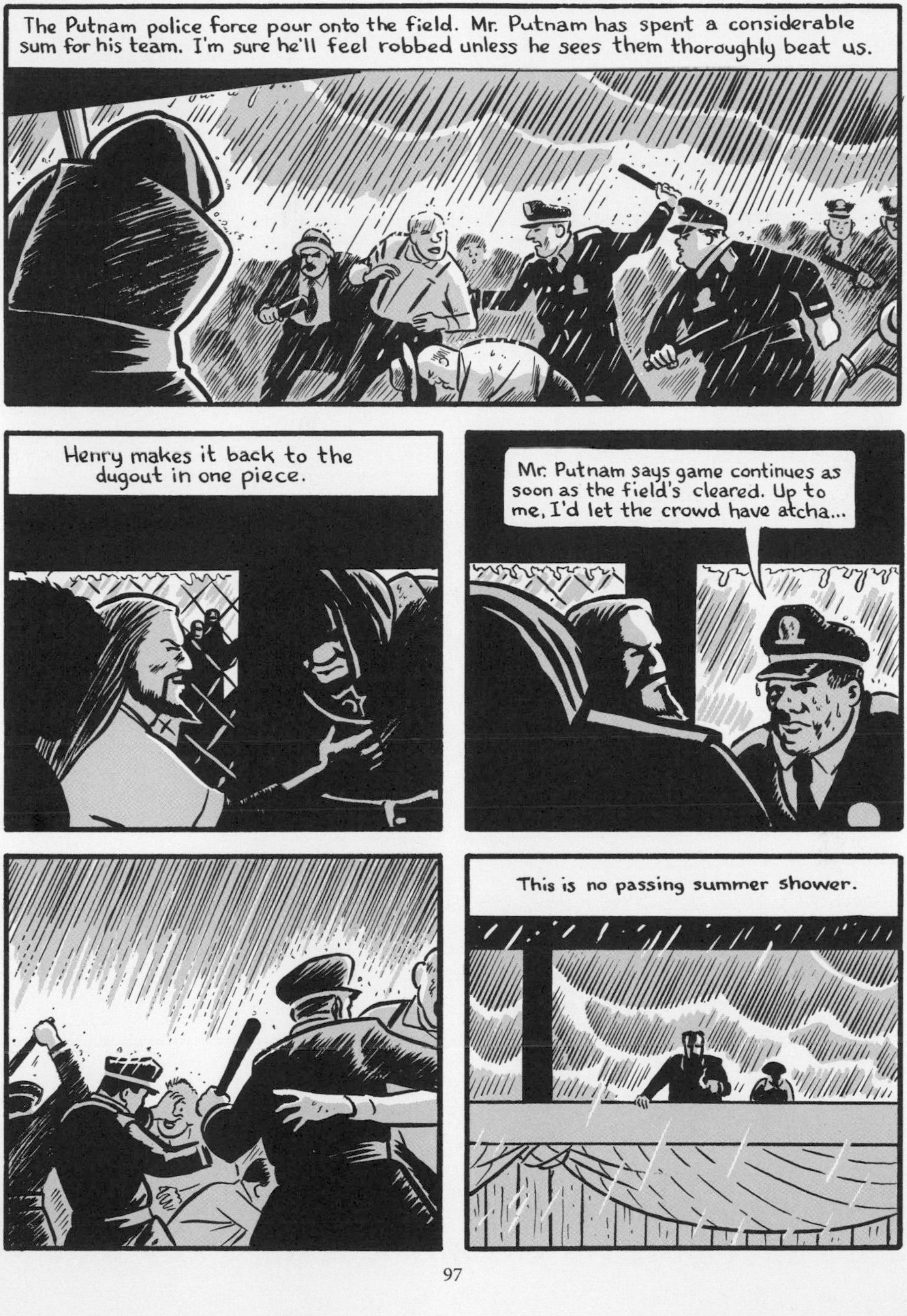
The Putnam police force pour onto the field. Mr. Putnam has spent a considerable sum for his team. I'm sure he'll feel robbed unless he sees them thoroughly beat us.
Henry makes it back to the dugout in one piece.
Mr. Putnam says game continues as soon as the field's cleared. Up to me, I'd let the crowd have atcha...
This is no passing summer shower.

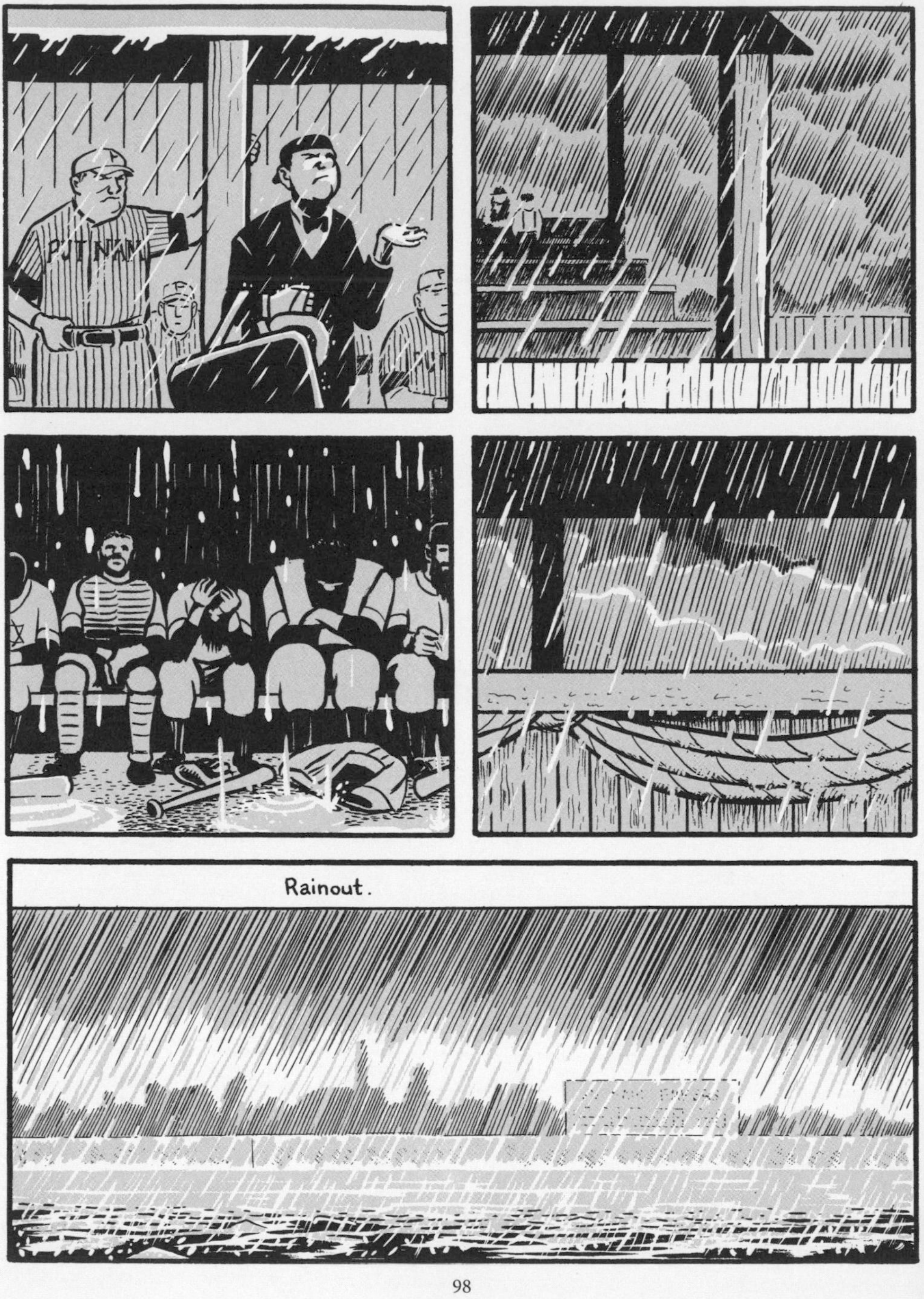
Rainout.

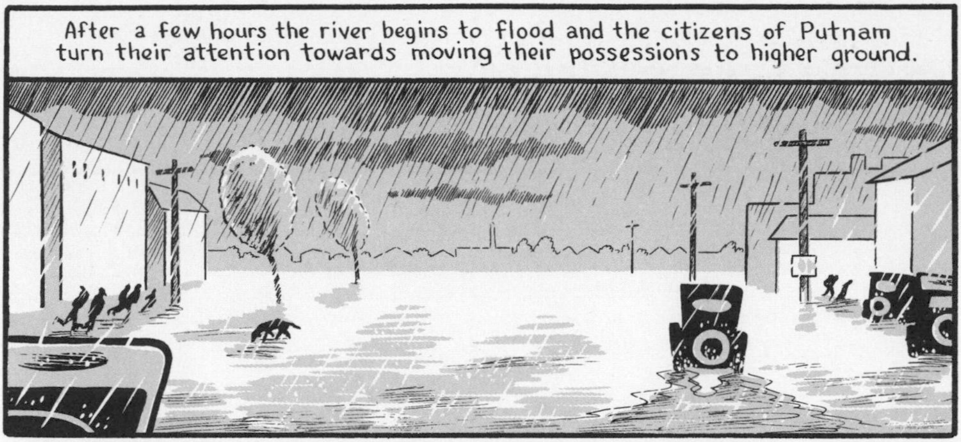
After a few hours the river begins to flood and the citizens of Putnam turn their attention towards moving their possessions to higher ground.

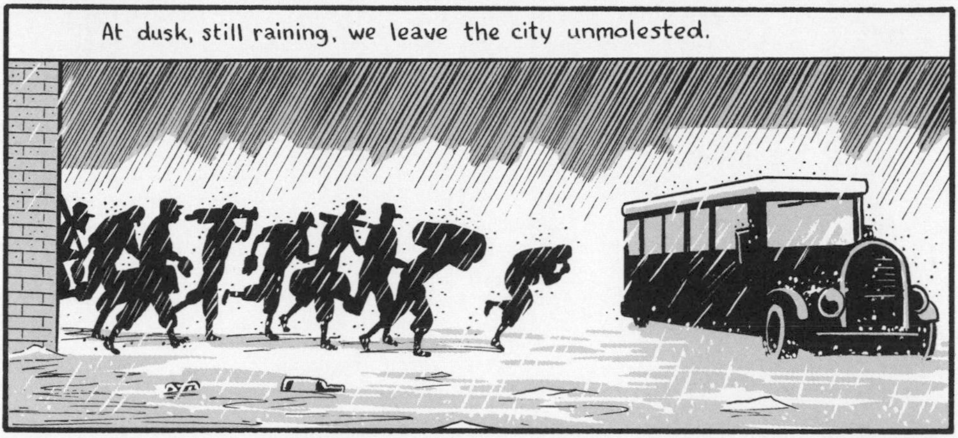
At dusk, still raining, we leave the city unmolested.

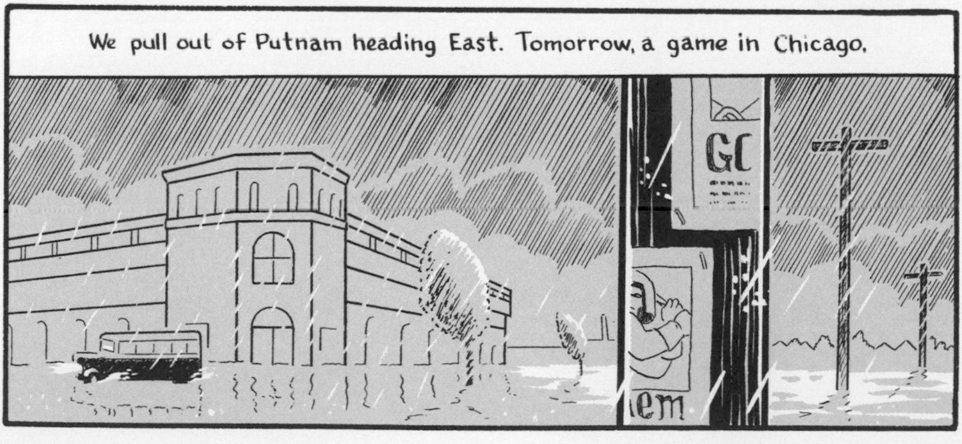
We pull out of Putnam heading East. Tomorrow, a game in Chicago.

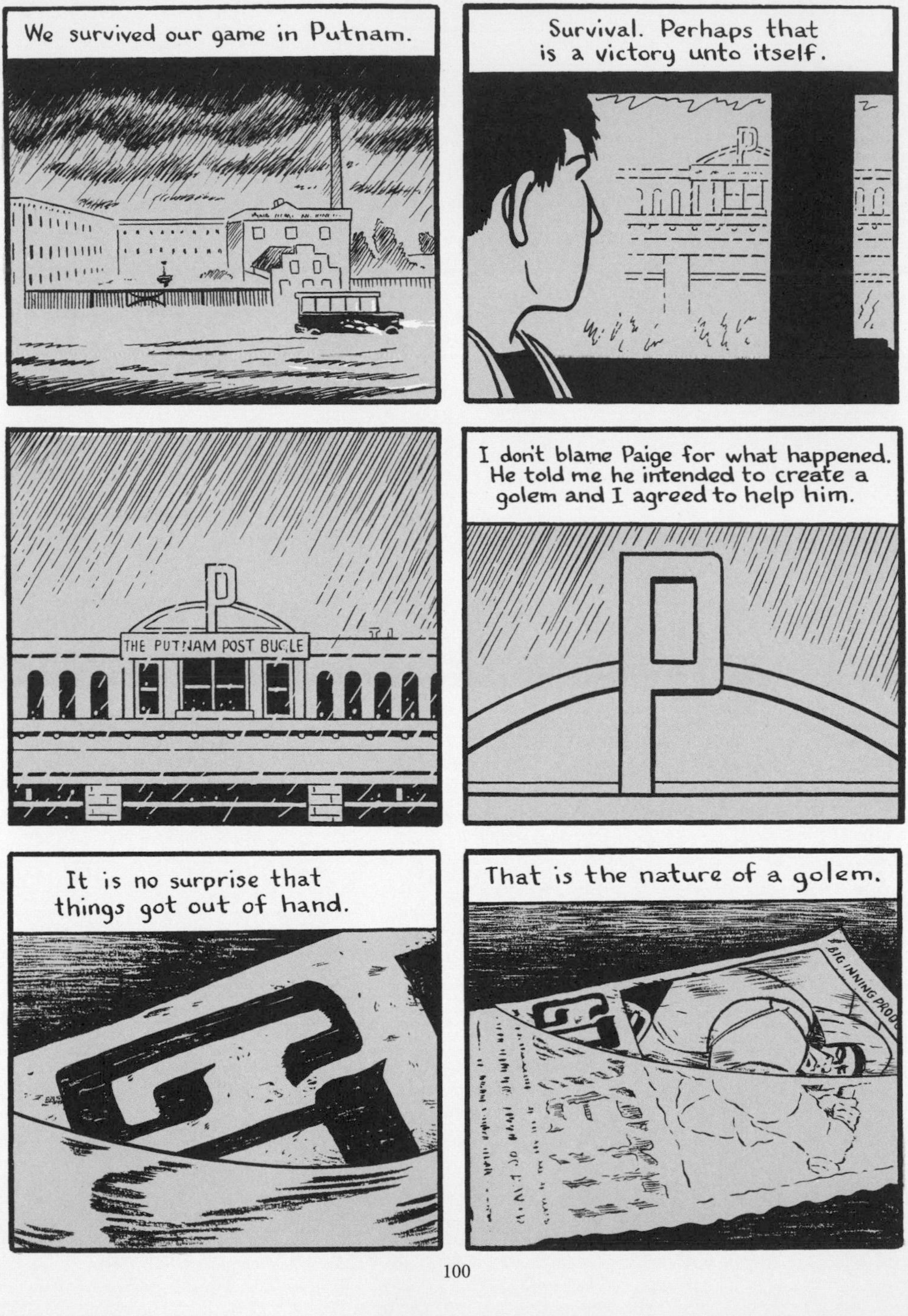
We survived our game in Putnam.
Survival. Perhaps that is a victory unto itself.
THE PUTNAM POST BUGLE
I don't blame Paige for what happened. He told me he intended to create a golem and I agreed to help him.
It is no surprise that things got out of hand.
That is the nature of a golem.

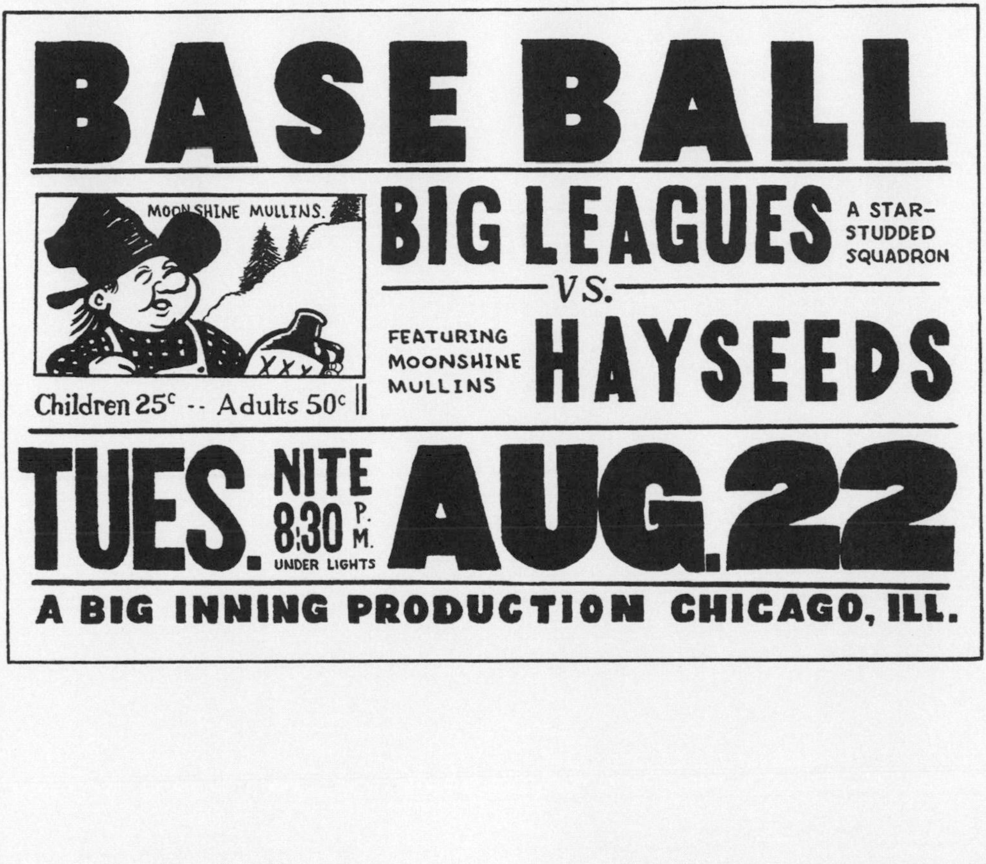
BASE BALL
MOONSHINE MULLINS.
XXX
BIG LEAGUES
A STAR-STUDDED SQUADRON
VS.
FEATURING MOONSHINE MULLINS
HAYSEEDS
Children 25c -- Adults 50c
TUES.
NITE 8:30 P.M.
UNDER LIGHTS
AUG. 22
A BIG INNING PRODUCTION CHICAGO, ILL.

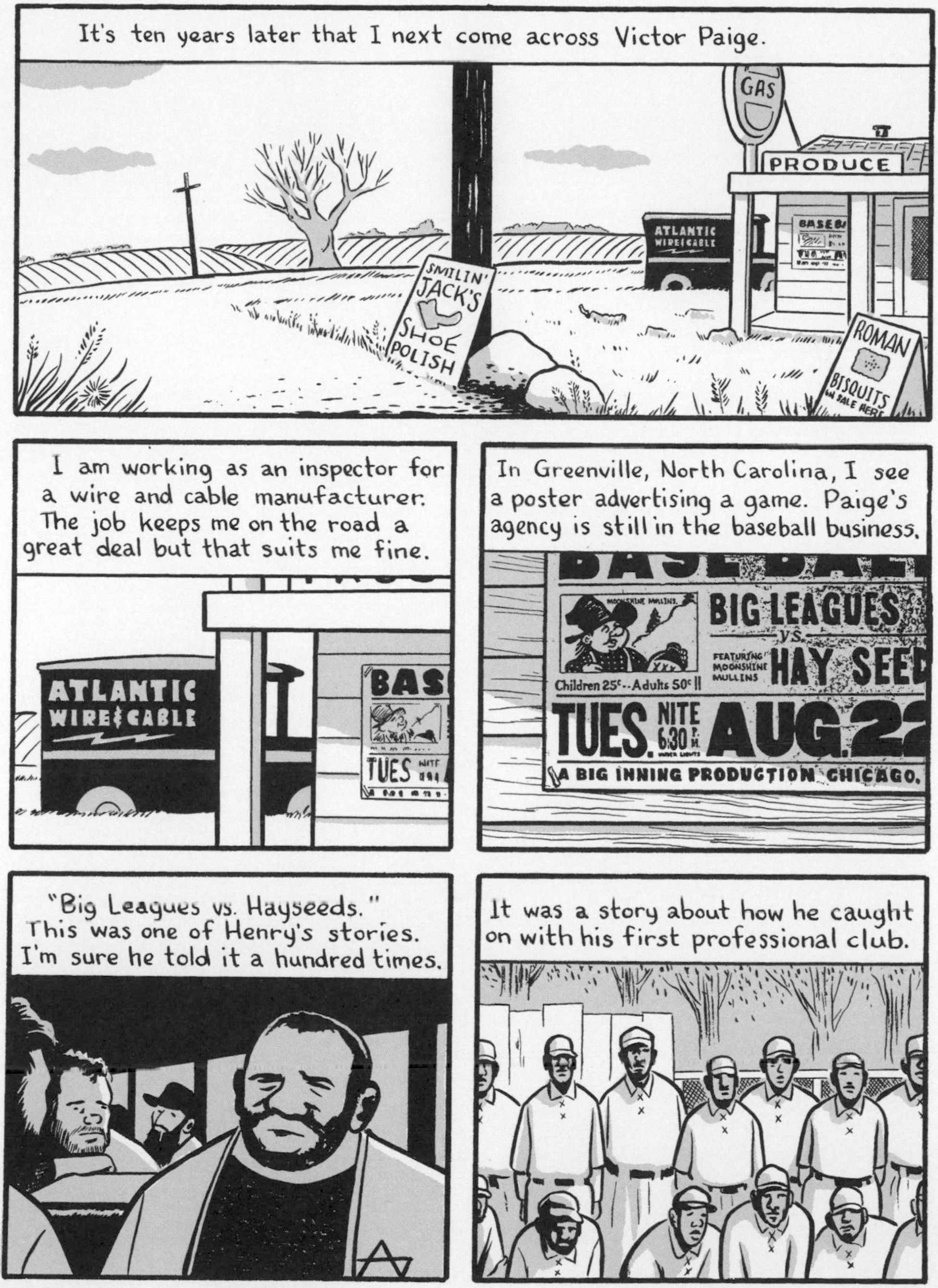
It's ten years later that I next come across Victor Paige.
GAS
PRODUCE
ATLANTIC WIRE & CABLE
SMILIN' JACK'S SHOE POLISH
ROMAN BISQUITS ON SALE HERE
I am working as an inspector for a wire and cable manufacturer. The job keeps me on the road a great deal but that suits me fine.
ATLANTIC WIRE & CABLE
In Greenville, North Carolina, I see a poster advertising a game. Paige's agency is still in the baseball business.
MOONSHINE MULLINS
BIG LEAGUES vs. HAY SEED
FEATURING MOONSHINE MULLINS
Children 25¢ - Adults 50¢
TUES. NITE 6:30 P.M.
AUG. 22
A BIG INNING PRODUCTION CHICAGO.
"Big Leagues vs. Hayseeds." This was one of Henry's stories. I'm sure he told it a hundred times.
It was a story about how he caught on with his first professional club.

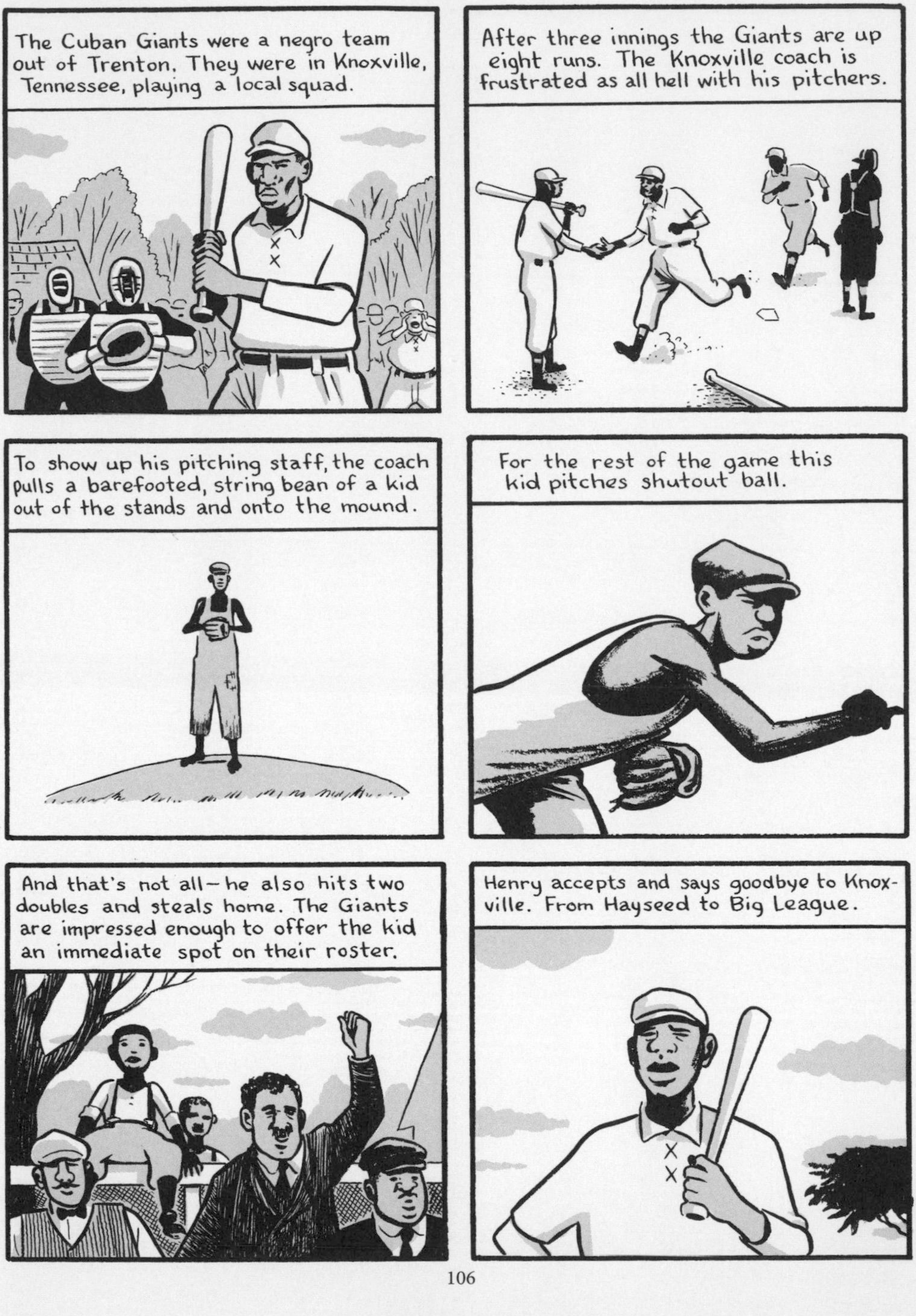
The Cuban Giants were a negro team out of Trenton. They were in Knoxville, Tennessee, playing a local squad.
After three innings the Giants are up eight runs. The Knoxville coach is frustrated as all hell with his pitchers.
To show up his pitching staff, the coach pulls a barefooted, string bean of a kid out of the stands and onto the mound.
For the rest of the game this kid pitches shutout ball.
And that's not all—he also hits two doubles and steals home. The Giants are impressed enough to offer the kid an immediate spot on their roster.
Henry accepts and says goodbye to Knoxville. From Hayseed to Big League.

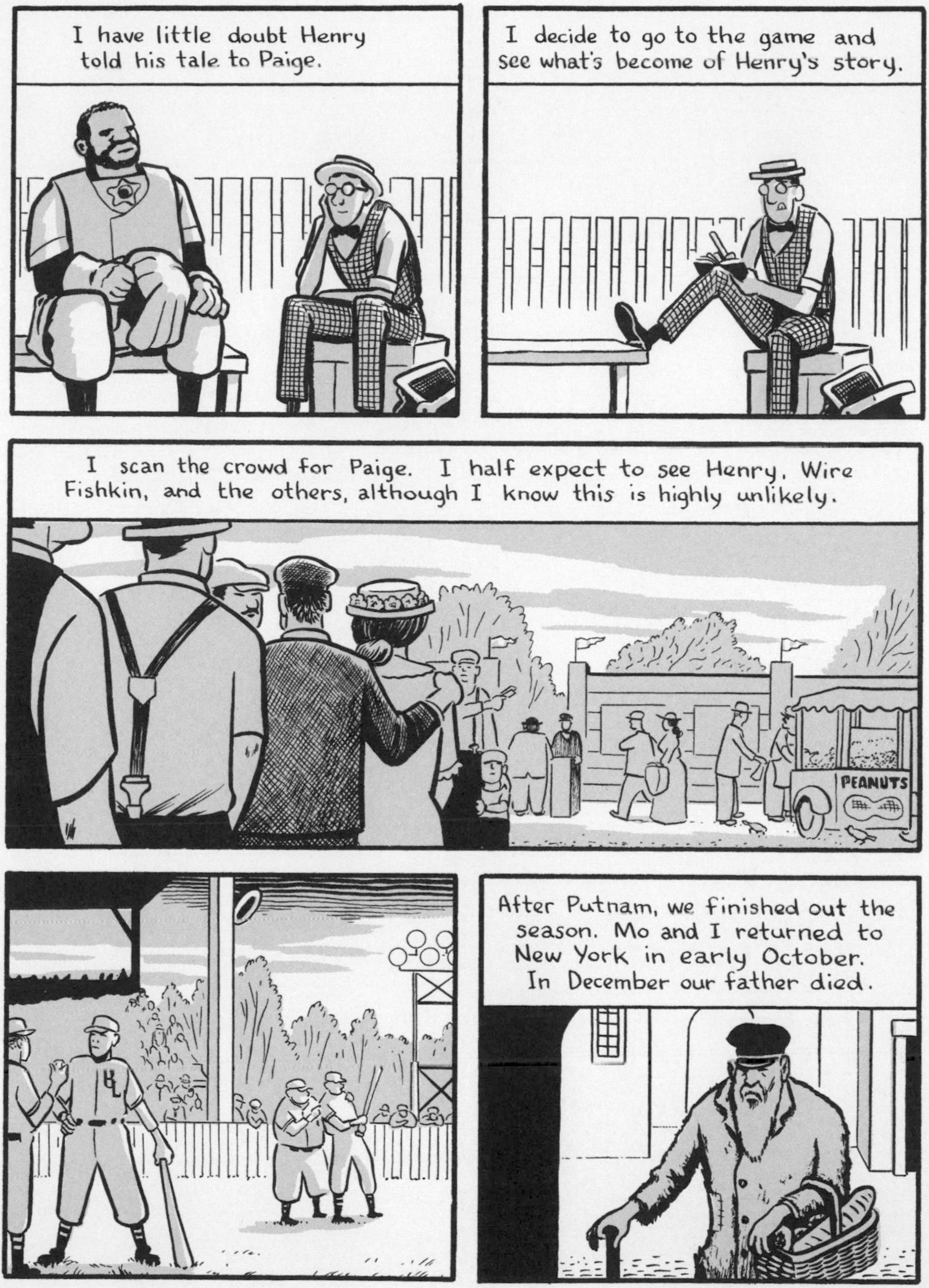
I have little doubt Henry told his tale to Paige.
I decide to go to the game and see what's become of Henry's story.
I scan the crowd for Paige. I half expect to see Henry, Wire Fishkin, and the others, although I know this is highly unlikely.
PEANUTS
After Putnam, we finished out the season. Mo and I returned to New York in early October. In December our father died.

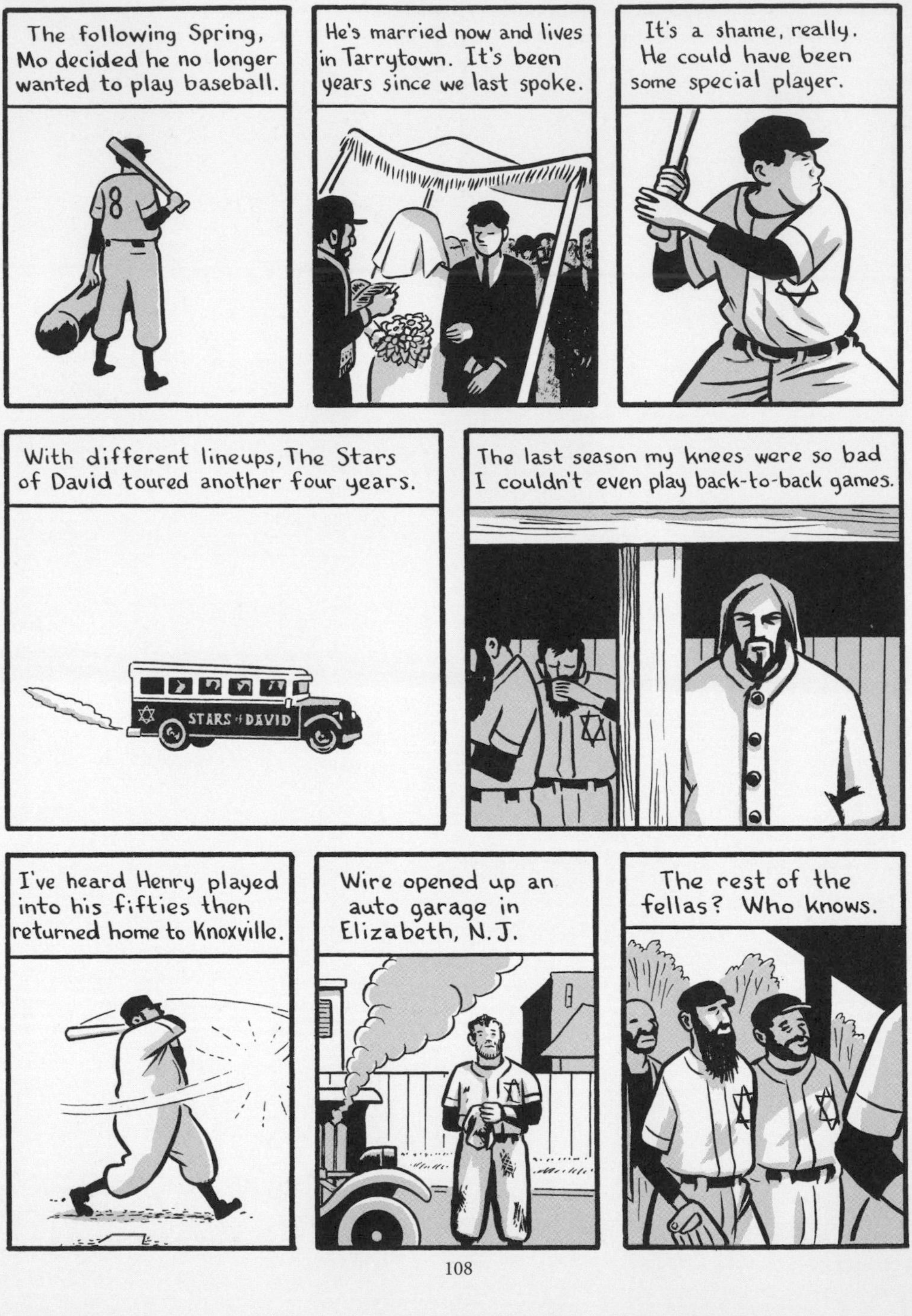
The following Spring, Mo decided he no longer wanted to play baseball.
He's married now and lives in Tarrytown. It's been years since we last spoke.
It's a shame, really. He could have been some special player.
With different lineups, The Stars of David toured another four years.
STARS of DAVID
The last season my knees were so bad I couldn't even play back-to-back games.
I've heard Henry played into his fifties then returned home to Knoxville.
Wire opened up an auto garage in Elizabeth, N.J.
The rest of the fellas? Who knows.

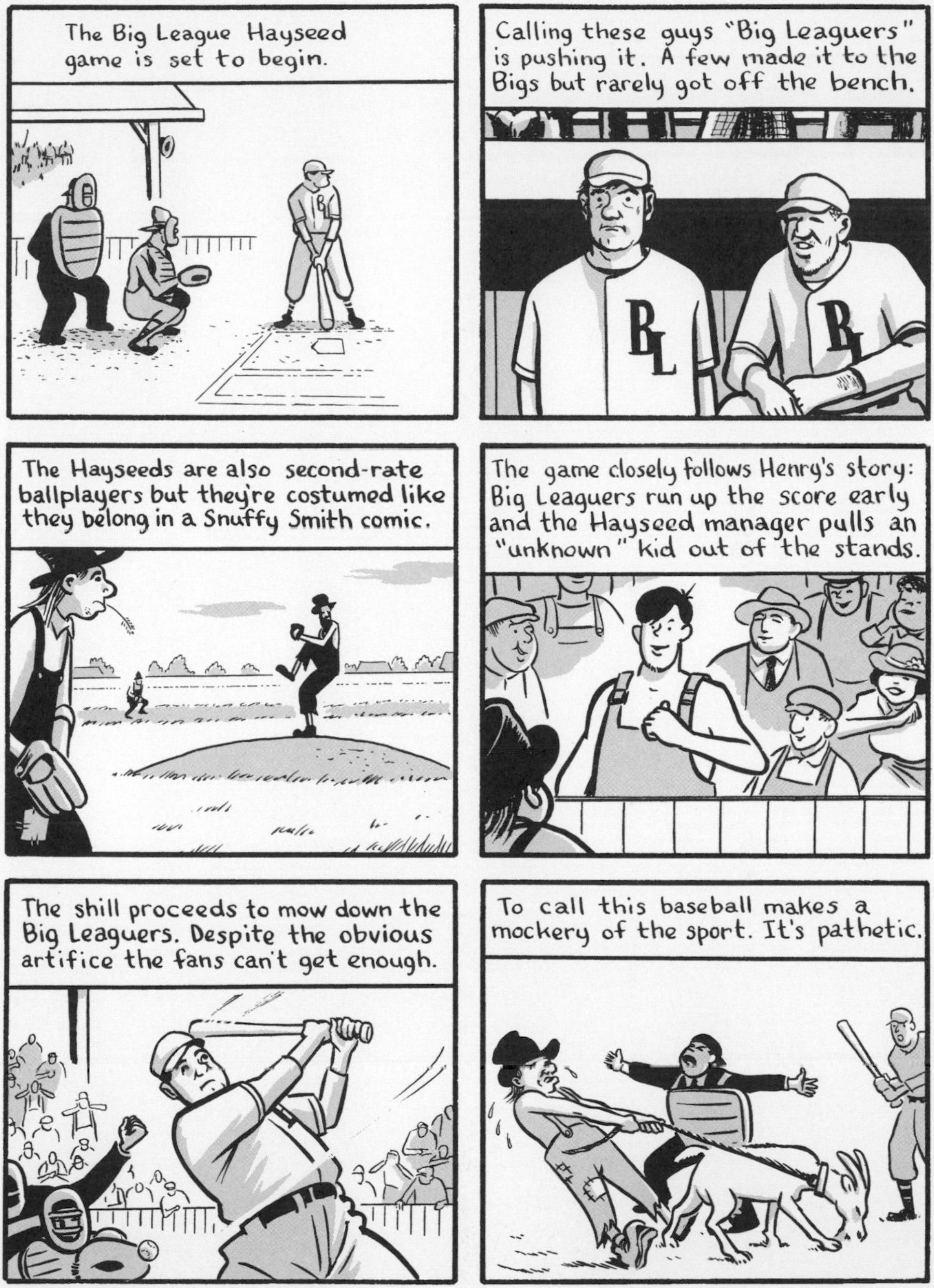
The Big League Hayseed game is set to begin.
Calling these guys "Big Leaguers" is pushing it. A few made it to the Bigs but rarely got off the bench.
The Hayseeds are also second-rate ballplayers but they're costumed like they belong in a Snuffy Smith comic.
The game closely follows Henry's story: Big Leaguers run up the score early and the Hayseed manager pulls an "unknown" kid out of the stands.
The shill proceeds to mow down the Big Leaguers. Despite the obvious artifice the fans can't get enough.
To call this baseball makes a mockery of the sport. It's pathetic.

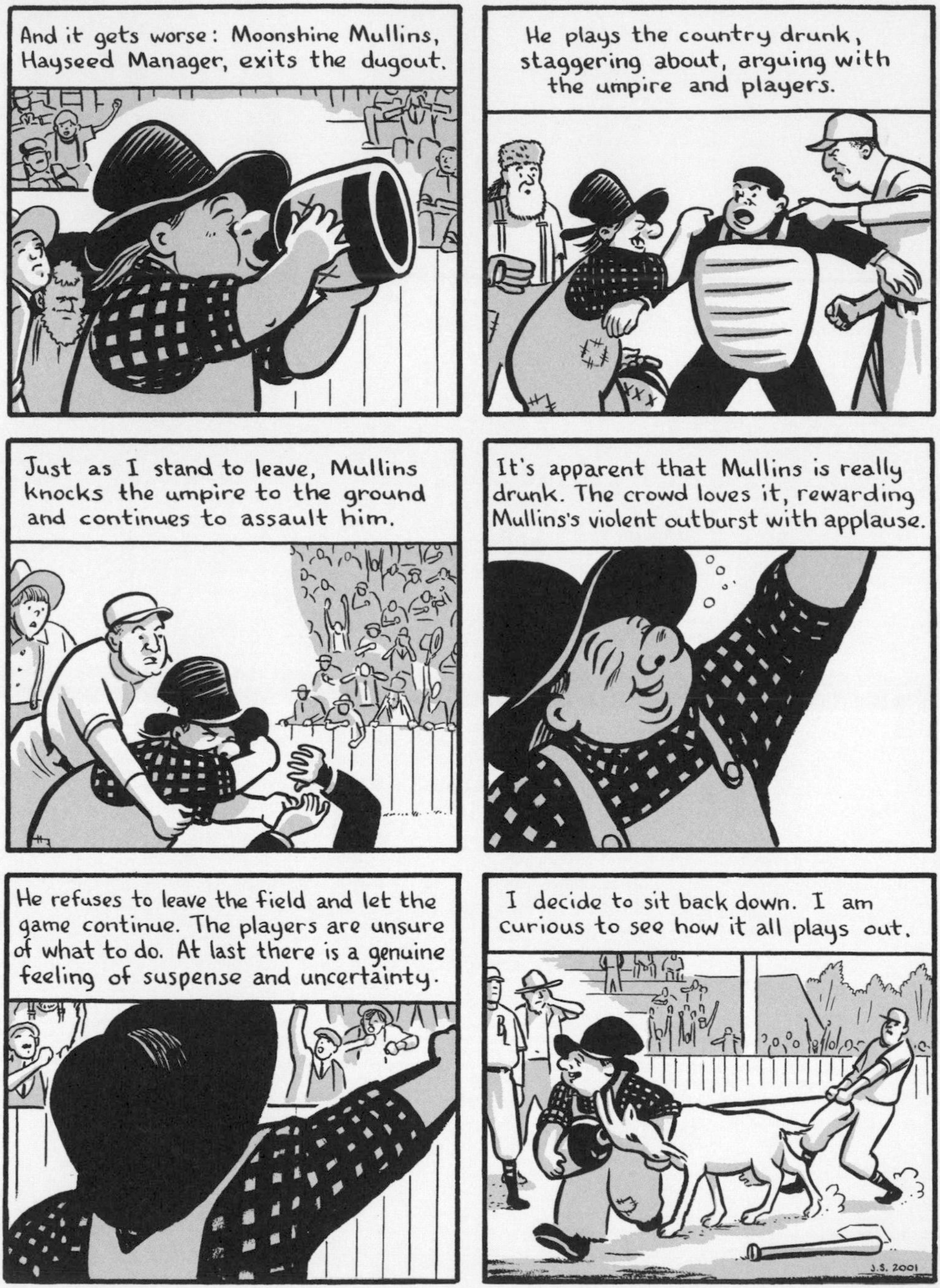
And it gets worse: Moonshine Mullins, Hayseed Manager, exits the dugout.
He plays the country drunk, staggering about, arguing with the umpire and players.
Just as I stand to leave, Mullins knocks the umpire to the ground and continues to assault him.
It's apparent that Mullins is really drunk. The crowd loves it, rewarding Mullins's violent outburst with applause.
He refuses to leave the field and let the game continue. The players are unsure of what to do. At last there is a genuine feeling of suspense and uncertainty.
I decide to sit back down. I am curious to see how it all plays out.
J.S. 2001